Inside
Japan

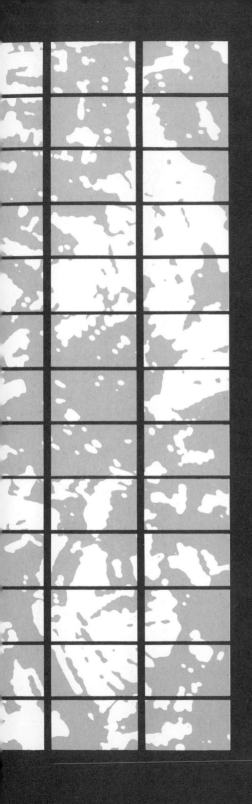

Have a great birthday Anil
My friend.

Always take care of yourself
wherever you May go!

Arshid

Inside Japan

British Broadcasting Corporation

This book is published to accompany
a series of BBC Television programmes first broadcast
on BBC 1 January 1980

Series producer: Howard Smith who also edited this book

Jacket photograph
Scene in the gardens of the Imperial Villa at Katsura in Kyōto

Published to accompany a series of programmes prepared in
consultation with the BBC Continuing Education Advisory Council

Text © 1981 by the Authors
First published 1981
Published by the British Broadcasting Corporation
35 Marylebone High Street, London W1M 4AA

Typeset by CCC, printed and bound in Great Britain by William Clowes
(Beccles) Limited, Beccles and London
This book is typeset in APS Clowes Dante 10pt leaded 2pts
ISBN 0 563 16300 3

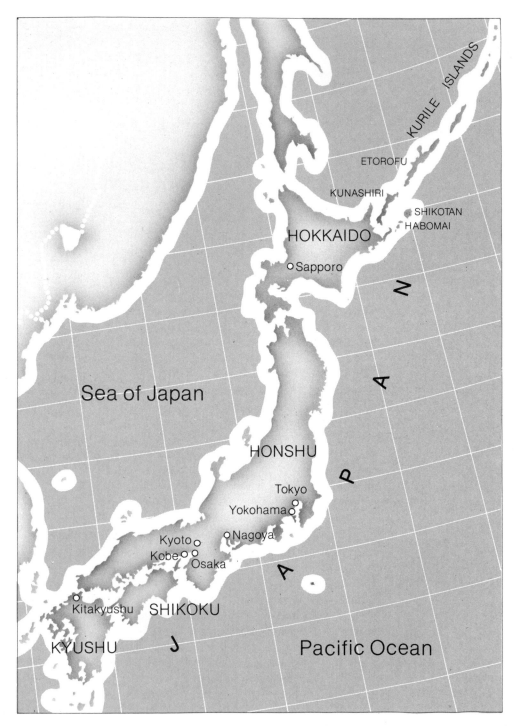

Introduction

Howard Smith

The six essays in this book have been written to provide a general background to the more important features of life in contemporary Japan. In view of its significance in the world today, it is surprising how little is really known about Japan and how much of this knowledge is still based either on prejudice or on outdated stereotypes. One of the main aims of this book is to dispel some of these misconceptions.

The book's other main objective is to try to get beneath the surface of Japanese life, and to look at the attitudes and values that the Japanese themselves take for granted but which are little known, let alone understood, in the outside world. In the opening essay Martin Collick looks at various significant features of contemporary society – the family, the company, the neighbourhood – and at attitudes to education and social welfare. Richard Boyd then investigates how far – in spite of the considerable changes that have taken place on the surface of society – young people are really different from their parents. In the third essay Geoffrey Bownas describes how, for many hundreds of years, cultural influences from outside Japan have been absorbed into the country's strong national tradition, and how this process continues today. Douglas Anthony's essay on the Japanese economy concentrates on the continuing significance of small firms in Japanese industry, their relationship with large firms, and the ways in which groups of large firms operate; in Graham Healey's analysis of the Japanese political system, the emphasis is on parties and elections, and especially on the significance of the factions inside the ruling Liberal Democratic Party; and in the final essay Gordon Daniels surveys Japan's relations with the outside world.

The Japanese themselves frequently make a point of emphasising to Western visitors those features of their society – the free market economy, political democracy – which they feel they share with countries in

North America and Western Europe. But simply to emphasise those features of their society which the Japanese have in common with other industrialised countries is to risk a fundamental misunderstanding of this fascinating and complex people. Just beneath the surface of life in Japan, which seen.s in many ways so like the West, there flourishes a very different society whose values are also significantly different from our own. If this book helps the reader to understand some of these differences it will have achieved its purpose.

The book follows the Japanese convention of giving the surname first and the personal name second.

I
A different society

Martin Collick

Introduction

There are two kinds of problem in writing about Japanese society. One is the nature of the subject. In a sense the whole of this book is about Japanese society, so that the decision to include any particular topic in this chapter rather than elsewhere is necessarily somewhat arbitrary. I have therefore chosen to concentrate on a few subjects which seem to me to be significant for a proper understanding of contemporary Japan.

The second, and far more basic problem, is a result of the nature of Japanese society. One of the most common approaches in any introduction of Japanese society to Western readers is to point to the very great contrasts between its 'traditional' and its 'modern' aspects. Tokyo and other large Japanese cities, it is pointed out, are as 'modern' as any in the world, with motorways, large hotels, factories using the most advanced technology, and mammoth new housing estates. On the other hand, the society retains many 'traditional' features, both material – ancient temples, traditional art forms, habits of dress, and so on – and intangible – ways of thinking, patterns of behaviour, and social relationships.

These contrasts are often explained by saying that the pace of change in Japan has been so fast that 'traditional' attitudes and patterns of behaviour have been unable to keep up with the 'modern' aspects of society – industry, technology, the education system or Western-style parliamentary government. This is a very neat way of explaining many of the peculiar features of Japanese society so that they are easily comprehensible to the Western reader, but it is at best superficial, and at worst liable to give an entirely misleading impression of postwar Japanese society. It assumes that 'modernisation' is a single universal process through which all societies pass – a sort of escalator leading from 'traditional' to 'modern' society – and that the differences between societies are simply the result of their different positions on this escalator.

This assumption may be acceptable when one is dealing with societies which have roughly the same sort of starting-point in terms of attitudes and values (the 'Christian' countries of Western Europe and North America, for example), but it quite clearly does not fit the case of Japan. Industrialisation and urbanisation have produced, and are continuing to produce, a society in Japan which is quite different from the society created by the same processes in the West. We are likely to understand this society better if we abandon terms like 'traditional' and 'modern', which carry with them all sorts of Western-based preconceptions, and simply accept that Japan is a *different* society, which has to be analysed and understood on its own terms.

In the West, industrialisation and the accompanying movement of population from the countryside to the cities largely broke down the traditional ties of rural society. In the pre-industrial society almost all a man's life – at work, at play, and at worship – had been spent in the company of a single group of people, all known to him, and with whom he identified almost completely. All his loyalties were given to this one group. In the new, urban society, however, a man is an independent individual, associating with a wide variety of different groups, depending on what he is doing at any particular moment. He identifies with none of them entirely; his loyalties are diverse, and often directed towards wider groups like 'the working class' or 'the Catholic Church' or towards abstract ideals like 'socialism', 'justice', or 'democracy'.

In Japan too there has been a massive flow of population from the land and into the cities in the last century or so, and particularly in the period since the Second World War. Less than seven per cent of the population now depend on agriculture for more than half their income, whilst more than half the total population of Japan now lives in cities with a population of 100,000 or more. On the whole, however, industrialisation and urbanisation have not brought about the sort of changes described in the previous paragraph. What has happened instead is that in urban Japan a variety of groups has been formed which reproduce, as it were, the conditions which existed in the village communities of the pre-industrial society. In employment, in residential areas, in politics, sport, the entertainment industry, and at leisure, the urban Japanese of today forms small 'family-like' groups with a clearly established hierarchy, under a leader who acts as 'father-figure' to the group. Once he has joined such a group, the individual tends to treat it as the framework for all his activities, and give it all his loyalties. His interests tend to be subordinated to (or rather regarded as identical with) those of the group, so that in his relations with the outside world he functions not as an independent individual making independent decisions on the basis of generally accepted norms, but in his capacity as a member of the group, on the basis of what will best serve the group's interests. So pervasive is the group-based organisation of Japanese society that the average Japanese finds it difficult to make decisions and to act in any other way.

We therefore have in contemporary Japan an apparently modern society made up of individuals whose behaviour and attitudes fit a pattern that is supposed to be typical of *traditional* societies. Nor is there any real evidence that this phenomenon is simply the product of a transitional phase – an example of 'culture lag' caused by the extremely rapid pace of Japanese industrialisation. Any 'modern' institution imported from abroad and any new movement arising within Japan itself tends to be gradually but surely adapted to fit this predominantly group-oriented pattern. It is likely to be more profitable, therefore, to examine Japanese society in terms of the various groups of which it is composed, rather than through concepts such as 'traditional' or 'modern', which tend to obscure rather than clarify important features of the society.

The Village

It would be rather strange, when writing about most industrial societies, to begin with a description of rural communities, which are by definition no longer in the mainstream of life in those societies. In a sense, of course, this is true of Japan, as the figures given in the introduction should indicate; Japan is now predominantly an urban society. Nevertheless, in that the group which forms the basis of social life in all sectors of Japanese society is essentially an extension of the traditional organisation of the village, a discussion of that organisation and of the changes that have taken place within it makes a convenient starting-point for a discussion of the society as a whole.

The farming village of pre-war Japan was a close-knit community, centring on and controlled by a small number of landlords and rich owner-farmers. Although they were able to exercise this leadership by virtue of their superior economic position, the situation was *not* one in which a large number of poverty-stricken tenant-farmers was ruled and exploited by a minute *rentier* class, as is still the case, for example, in much of Latin America. Although there were considerable regional differences throughout the country, in the typical Japanese village there was no such clear dividing-line between the very rich and the very poor, but rather a fairly subtle, though clearly perceived, graduation of economic status. Large-scale absentee landlords were few; the majority of landlords were also owner-farmers, and some were also tenants. The typical pattern was for farmers to cultivate both their own and rented land, in varying proportions. Secondly, naked economic domination was the exception rather than the rule. Leadership was exercised on the basis

Left
Twenty years ago, when rice was still being planted by hand, it took a man and his family between fifty and sixty days a year to cultivate one acre of rice.

Right
Today, with the aid of machinery, it takes about half this time.

of tradition and, indeed, it was quite common for a family to retain its high status within the village for some time after the purely economic reason for that status had been lost. Finally, and perhaps most important, the village was thought of as essentially a co-operative unit, in which interests common to the whole village, landlord and tenant alike, predominated in everyday life over those of any *section* of the community. The village often held woodland in common, and both the control of water for irrigation, and the intensive seasonal labour involved in wet-field rice agriculture, were enterprises requiring the co-operation of all members of the village. Disputes with neighbouring communities over rights to woodlands and water were common, and served to emphasise the solidarity of the village in its relations with the outside world.

After the Second World War the Occupation authorities saw the domination of rural society by the landlord class as one of the major obstacles to the democratisation of Japanese society. They therefore instituted a programme of land reform which transferred the ownership of virtually all tenanted agricultural land from the landlords to the tenants, effectively turning the whole of the Japanese farming population into small-scale owner-cultivators.

Even in pre-war Japan, the majority of Japanese farming families found it necessary to supplement their income from the land, either by seasonal handicraft work, or by a member of the family leaving the village temporarily to work in industry. After the war, however, the rapid development of industry created a severe shortage of labour and an increase in industrial wage rates which drew an increasing proportion of the male population of the farming village to abandon agriculture altogether, and seek permanent employment in the cities, or in the

*Traditional crafts
still survive in
the countryside.
Making baskets
from local bamboo
in the village of
Kurotsuchi.*

factories which have increasingly spread into the countryside. As a result, about two-thirds of Japanese farms are now entirely dependent on the labour of the female members of the family.

The land reforms destroyed the economic basis for the domination of the village by the landlords and large owner-farmers. Moreover, the predominance of non-agricultural occupations as the main source of income in the countryside, and the large number of men who have gone off to work in the towns, leaving their wives and parents to run the farm – returning themselves only at night or at weekends – have created a diversity of interests within the village which did not exist when it was a virtually self-contained agricultural community. Post-war reorganisation of the Local Government system, moreover, has submerged what had been identifiable separate communities in larger administrative units, further weakening their sense of corporate identity.

Despite these changes, however, long tradition and the continuing
needs of the Japanese system of rice farming have kept alive the sense of
solidarity and common interest. The old Neighbourhood Association
may have been replaced by the Agricultural Co-operative as the focus for
village activity, but this activity is still overwhelmingly directed towards
the interests of the village, rather than those of the new, larger administrative units, or of occupational or other groups organised on a scale
larger than that of the village. This fact in its turn has meant that political
activity tends to be organised on a village basis, with villages supporting
candidates who appear likely to further their own interest, and candidates
reciprocating with favours when elected.

In spite of the fact that the population of Japan is now predominantly
urban, many Japanese retain close ties – emotional at least – with the
rural areas in which they or their parents originated. Ask a Japanese
where he comes from, and the chances are that he will give you the name
of some rural prefecture, from which his parents 'emigrated' well before
he was born. More important, however, for a consideration of Japanese
society as a whole is the fact that the attitudes developed in the environment of the rural village have been transferred with little change to that
of the city. To the rural Japanese the world outside his own small
community was (and is) of little importance. All his interests and activities were concentrated within the village, and events outside were
significant only in so far as they directly affected the village in some way.
In industrial, urban Japan, the village has been replaced by a variety of
different groups, but the attitude of the individual to whatever group
forms the focus of his loyalty is virtually identical with that which
formed the basis of life in the rural community.

The Firm

For a large number of Japanese men the firm in which they are employed
forms the basis for the group on which their lives are centred. Japanese
industrial organisations have often been referred to as 'family enterprises', and although this label is useful because it emphasises the strongly
emotional nature of the relationship between the worker and the firm
for which he works, it can also mask the very real differences in this
relationship, which depend on the size and type of firm and the individual's position within it.

In large-scale private industry, public corporations, and the Civil
Service, the typical pattern of employment is that a worker joins the
organisation immediately on completing full-time education, and
spends the whole of his working life there. In return for his loyalty to the
firm, expressed in a willingness not to seek employment elsewhere, and
to serve the firm in whatever capacity and in whatever part of Japan or

the world it chooses to use him, he receives virtually absolute security of employment, and a variety of other benefits. His salary will normally rise throughout his working life in rough proportion to his needs and rising status within the firm, and is not based directly on his performance. He will also receive increases in pay as his family commitments increase, as well as a lump-sum retirement benefit, a good pension, and membership of the firm's health insurance scheme. The company may well provide him with subsidised accommodation – in a company hostel until he marries, and then in a company house.

The relationship described so far is a relatively impersonal one, between an individual employee on the one hand and a large organisation on the other, and as such hardly warrants the description 'family-like'. In his day-to-day working life, however, the employee is a member of a small group, formed of workers in the same office or workshop. It is through his membership of this group, the sense of identification with it, and the loyalty that he feels for it, that his identification with and loyalty to the larger group is expressed. It is this smaller group that is the equivalent in industrial life of the family-like society of the village, and within which the individual functions in the majority of his everyday activities. If he goes out for a drink after work, or fishing at the weekend, the chances are that it will be in the company of the people with whom he spends his working day. If he takes part in sports, it is likely to be with his workmates and probably on the firm's sports ground, or at a golf club at which the company has arranged (and paid for) his membership. His immediate superior at work (as 'father-figure' of the family group) will quite likely be asked for advice and assistance in such personal matters as

Company housing for workers at Mitsubishi Motors in Kyōto.

Athletics Day at the Tochigi plant of the Nissan Motor Company.

finding a suitable wife, or jobs for his children, and will offer this sort of advice unasked if he feels it necessary in order to preserve or strengthen the employee's loyalty to the group, and his identification with it.

Even so, in a large organisation, there are limits to the extent to which the relationship between employer and employee can be represented in personal, 'family', terms, even within the small workplace group. The provisions made by a company for its employees, and the care shown by a superior for his subordinates, clearly contain a large element of role-playing. They are instruments of company policy, designed to strengthen the relationship, and the employee is well aware of this fact. It is very rare, however, for him to regard them as in any way objectionable – as restricting his freedom or interfering in his private life. Neither freedom nor privacy in this sense are concepts on which he places a very high value, certainly not in comparison with security. He too is to some extent playing a role. He will arrive early at work and leave late, and rarely takes anything like the number of days' holiday to which he is entitled. Even if his wife is expecting him home for dinner he will go to a bar after work with his colleagues, and will sacrifice his Sundays at home with the family without demur if company business (or socialising with his colleagues) requires it. He is quite often deliberately going out of his way to prove his loyalty, to show that he regards the employment relationship as taking precedence over all else. But as time passes, and the worker's status in the group is established, the element of conscious role-playing diminishes, and demonstrations of loyalty become a way of life. The loyalty is now entirely genuine. A large majority of Japanese male workers – particularly office workers in large organisations – when asked where they find their major source of satisfaction in life, will answer not 'at home', or 'in leisure', but 'at work'.

The picture painted above is often regarded, by Japanese as well as foreigners, as typical of the relationship between the Japanese worker and the firm that employs him. There are, however, several qualifications which need to be introduced. The first is the fact that this sort of relationship, and the attitudes that underlie it, exists only for a minority of the Japanese work-force – permanent male employees of large industrial and commercial firms, and local and central government.

Well over two-thirds of the Japanese labour force are employed by firms with less than 500 workers. On the one hand the small firm, often under-capitalised, inefficient, and working to lower profit margins than its larger counterparts, is simply unable to emulate them in terms of the benefits that it offers to its employees. In this smaller sector company housing is the exception rather than the rule, though some firms will provide hostel accommodation for some of their workers. Small firms cannot afford to provide sports grounds or other recreational facilities, nor, what is more important, can they provide the sort of generous medical insurance or superannuation schemes which are normal in large companies. Some of the more prosperous small firms take part in co-operative welfare schemes operated by a number of firms in the same industry or geographical area, but these are the exception rather than the rule, and the majority of workers in small-scale industry and commerce have no more than the legal minimum of cover.

But perhaps the most crucial difference is that smaller firms are far more exposed to variation in the economic climate than are large concerns, and because of this are unable to offer the security of lifetime employment which is the keystone of the system described earlier. Bankruptcies are common and labour turnover high. In fact the very existence of this sector of industry as suppliers and subcontractors to the larger firms enables the latter to offer security to their own employees. When times are bad these small suppliers are driven out of business and their employees out of work. Compensating to some extent for the fact that the small enterprise cannot offer a great deal of material security is the fact that its very smallness enables it to be far more nearly a genuine

The body assembly line at the Tochigi plant of the Nissan Motor Company. The plant manager discusses problems with the foreman in charge of one of the shifts.

'family enterprise'. The employee can identify with the firm itself on a personal level. The owner of the firm may well be working with him and, as well as drinking together in the evenings, employer and employees may well go on trips together at midsummer and before the New Year festival. The proprietor's interest in his workers is far less likely to be role-playing than is the case in the larger firms. The employment relationship is more of a genuine extension of the family-like relationships which existed in the farming village, and less of a conscious attempt to imitate them.

A second important qualification is that, even in the largest firms, it is normal for a proportion of the workforce to be temporary employees, with none of the security offered to their permanent workmates. Though employees of the company, they are not entitled to membership of the company union, nor to the other benefits received by permanent employees. They, like the small suppliers and subcontractors mentioned earlier, are in this sense 'expendable'. Since they can be discarded if business conditions deteriorate they act as a 'buffer' whose existence enables the large firms to offer lifetime employment on advantageous conditions to a privileged minority. It is for this reason that temporary workers are not normally admitted to the company union – their inter-

ests are essentially in conflict with those of the permanent members who form the main part of the workforce.

In a period of sustained and rapid growth, such as Japan has enjoyed for the last three decades, the basic inequalities of the system are not necessarily perceived as particularly unjust. For many temporary workers, or poorly-paid employees of small firms, the job they had was far more attractive than the even less well-paid life of a farmer that they had recently left. Moreover, the prospect of unemployment appeared remote; even if one job disappeared, there were plenty of others available in an economy where labour was in perpetually short supply. Even the temporary worker was given considerable security by the economic prosperity of the nation as a whole. Recently, however, the situation has changed quite dramatically. Japan appears to have entered what may be a long period of slow economic growth, and the temporary employee who loses his job, or the semi-skilled worker in a small firm which is forced out of business, is finding it increasingly difficult to find other employment. For virtually the first time since the end of the Occupation, these workers are faced with the prospect of – possibly long-term – unemployment on a scale which the nation's welfare system is not equipped to deal with.

The third group who have little place in the lifetime-employment system described earlier are women. Despite the guarantees of equality

Young women at the Atsugi plant of the Sony Corporation shopping during the lunchtime break.

in the post-war Japanese Constitution, women are discriminated against in all areas of employment. Except in a few professions, notably teaching, medicine, and to a lesser extent the Civil Service, it is virtually a condition of employment that a female white-collar worker must resign on marriage; even the woman who chooses a career instead of marriage is seldom given the opportunity to compete with her male colleagues on an equal basis, but will usually spend her working life in low-grade clerical work. The female manual worker is in a similar situation, and in the smaller firm her position is even less secure than that of her male colleagues, though to some extent her very 'sackability' and the low wages for which she is willing to work may mean that in a period of recession there will be *more* job opportunities at the bottom end of the scale for a woman than for a man.

In short, therefore, the relationship between the worker and the firm is far from forming a single clearly-defined system. It has as its basic constituents a pattern of inequality between different types of worker. For the last twenty-five years the defects of the system have been masked by seemingly permanent and rising prosperity, but they may present real problems if people's expectations can no longer be fulfilled.

Trades Unions

The process by which workers came to identify with the firms for which they worked began in the early stages of Japanese industrialisation at the end of the nineteenth century, and early in the twentieth. Throughout this period Japan's new industries suffered from a shortage of labour. Individual firms recruited workers straight from the countryside, housed them, and provided them with the other necessities of life. Workers brought with them their rural attitudes without having passed through a pool of urban unemployed, and without, therefore, the opportunity to develop a sense of community of interest with other members of a developing 'working class'. In order to hold on to scarce labour, firms offered incentives for long service, and deliberately fostered a sense of loyalty to the firm among their workers, representing the factory as the equivalent of the family, and the employer as an authoritarian but benevolent father. In this way identification with the firm pre-empted, as it were, identification with wider groups such as workers in the same craft or industry, or with the working class as a whole. Pre-war and wartime Governments encouraged this trend, regarding 'class' consciousness as destructive of national unity, when masters and men should instead be working together for the common good.

In the face of workers' apathy and Goverment repression, the pre-war trades union movement was largely ineffective. Even since the War, however, when workers in most industries have been free to organise

and strike, the effectiveness of the movement has been severely restricted – at least in terms of large-scale concerted action – by workers'
attitudes, which have changed little since the pre-war period, and by the
pattern of union organisation developed as a result of those attitudes.

Since the average Japanese worker identifies his interests most closely
with other employees in the same firm, regardless of their occupation–
that is, he sees himself as an employee of xyz Steel Company first and
foremost, only secondly as a welder, and rarely, if at all, as a member of
the working class – it is natural that the trades unions that he forms
should be organized on an 'enterprise' rather than a 'craft' or 'industrial'
basis, as is the common pattern in most Western countries. All the
permanent non-supervisory employees of a particular firm – or of each
plant in a firm – will be organised into a single union, which will have
no members from outside the firm. These enterprise or plant-wide
unions will be organised into industry-wide federations, which will
again be members of one of the national trades union centres – the
rough equivalent of Britain's TUC or the AFL – CIO of the United States.
Superficially, therefore, there exists a pattern not unlike that in other
industrialised countries, but with the crucial difference that in the West
the normal pattern is of a single national union with local branches,
whereas in Japan it is of a multiplicity of small autonomous unions, who
are members of national federations with little or no authority.

This type of union organisation has both weaknesses and strengths,
and one's evaluation of these will depend very much on one's general
view of the nature of the employment relationship. If it is regarded as a
relationship where conflict is inevitable – or even necessary, in order to
bring about basic changes in the structure of society – then the Japanese
pattern of union organisation must be a bad one, since it puts its
members, and the working class as a whole, at a severe disadvantage in
the struggle.

First of all, of course, employees in an enterprise-based union are
highly susceptible to arguments that industrial action would damage
the firm and therefore themselves. A union sees its main function as the
improvement of the wages and conditions of its own members, which
can best be achieved through negotiations with their own employer.
Even when there has been an agreement for concerted action on an
industry-wide basis, unions are easily 'picked off' in this way, so that
effective industrial action on a national scale is virtually impossible.

A second criticism of the system is that it blinds workers to their real
interests. By concentrating on relationships within the small world of
the enterprise, they are ignoring the wider struggle of the working class
as a whole. And it is true that the pattern of trades union organisation
gives unions little incentive to extend union membership into firms and
industries which are still unorganised. In the Japanese context the 'soli-

darity of the working class' is largely an empty phrase. The majority of workers find it difficult to identify with any group as large and nebulous as a class, and have little interest in improving the wages and conditions of other workers. The result is that only a small proportion of workers in small enterprises are organised into trades unions, despite the fact that their wages, working conditions and other benefits fall well below those in either public employment or large-scale private industry. This is perhaps the most serious failure of the Japanese trades union movement, making the claims of the leaders to be 'fighting for the whole working class' sound rather hollow.

A further criticism often levelled at the Japanese enterprise union is that it is no more than a 'company union' – a puppet – supported by the employer in a variety of ways, and whose main function is to ensure the compliance of the workforce with the policies and interests of the employer. Such unions certainly exist in Japan, but they are the exception rather than the rule. Apparent compliance with company wishes stems not from control by the company, but from a genuine belief on the part of the work-force that over a wide range of matters their interests and those of their employers are the same. Generally speaking – and the working class are no exception – the Japanese put a very high value on harmony in human relationships, and regard conflict as something to be avoided wherever possible. They have been helped towards this objective not only by a continuously expanding economy, which has made it easy for workers to achieve a rising standard of living without frequent recourse to industrial action, but also by the structure of the union movement itself. Since the movement's power is at the 'grass-roots' level, rather than in some distant headquarters in Tokyo, negotiations over local issues are far simpler, and far less likely to result in disputes, than if they had to wade through a cumbersome series of bureaucratic stages.

Furthermore, the union structure has made technological innovation far easier to achieve than has been the case in, say, Britain. The worker has no strong attachment to any particular craft, and so long as his employer will relocate him within the company –which has normally been possible in the rapidly expanding Japanese economy – he is quite happy to abandon his job as, say, a welder, and be retrained as electrician or lathe operator, without falling foul of craft unions who see their members being poached or their traditional craft preserves invaded.

Labour relations in the public sector are completely different. In contrast to the 'enterprise' unions typical of private industry, the employees of public corporations such as the National Railways, and civil servants such as teachers, are organised into national unions. They have no right to strike and only limited negotiating rights. Partly as a result of this, and partly because their employer – directly or indirectly – is the Government, they have become highly politicised, with a left-wing leadership which has indulged in continuous but fruitless ideological confrontation. This has created such an atmosphere of suspicion and hostility that a rational dialogue on any topic between Government and unions is almost impossible; and the consequences, notably in the field of education, have been very harmful.

On the whole, though, the organisation of Japan's trades union movement has served its members well. The enterprise union is a highly efficient and flexible bargaining unit, able to represent the views of its members far more effectively than a huge bureaucratic organisation. Whether it will be able to do so in the future is less certain; in a prolonged recession, where redundancies – even of permanent employees – would be inevitable, the unions would be torn between their desire to preserve the existence of the firm, and thus the jobs of at least *some* of their members, and their ingrained opposition to dismissals, which strike at the very basis of the lifetime employment system. The fiercest industrial disputes in post-war Japan have involved this very issue, which is likely to arise even more frequently in the future, and whether the trades unions can act effectively in such a situation will be a real test of the viability of the system.

The neighbourhood

There is, as we have seen, a considerable proportion of the urban Japanese population which is not employed either by the Government or in medium- or large-scale industry. For an industrialised country Japan still has an unusually high proportion of people operating very small-scale workshops and businesses, either alone, with the help of members of their immediate family, or with one or two employees. There are also the wives and families of workers in the larger-scale companies. For all these people it is the neighbourhood in which they live that forms the focus for their lives. Indeed, one of the most noticeable characteristics of the older areas of Japanese towns and cities has been the strong sense of neighbourhood solidarity, somewhat similar to that which used to be regarded as typical of the East End of London. Before and during the Second World War, Neighbourhood Associations – which had a long history already – were officially organised as the lowest level of state control to mobilise the population for the war effort. In many areas – particularly the older residential areas of Japanese cities – these organisations (or, rather, their direct descendants) still exist, on an autonomous rather than an official basis, but still serving to express and strengthen the community spirit of the neighbourhood. This community spirit is still very much in evidence, symbolised most clearly perhaps by the festival of the local shrine, in which the whole neighbourhood takes part, with the lead being taken by the members of the community

A Mikoshi, or portable shrine, at the Torigoe Festival in Tokyo's Asakusa district.

recognised as having high status within it – either by tradition, economic influence, force of personality, or a combination of these factors. These festivals are a precise parallel to those held in the countryside, where they have for centuries served as the symbol and focus of the solidarity and community of interest of the members of the village.

On the personal level too there is a strong sense of mutual interdependence, and an awareness of relative status within the community – which are also features of rural society. If a house in the neighbourhood is damaged by fire, for example, every household will contribute a 'sympathy gift' – usually of money, but sometimes of blankets or other

25

household necessities – the value of the gift being determined by the giver's status in the local community. If a member of the community dies the whole neighbourhood will be represented at the funeral, and the seating arrangements at the funeral dinner will again be determined by relative status in the community. (In all these cases it is the status of the member's *family* that counts; even at this level, the constituents of the group are not so much individuals as yet smaller groups – in this case families. It is by virtue of his membership of the smaller group that he is a member of the larger – a pattern repeated at all levels of society.)

All major stages in the life cycle – births, weddings, success in examinations, bereavements, and so on – are occasions for visits and presents of congratulation or sympathy, as are the major traditional festivals at midsummer and the New Year. The first act of a new resident in such a neighbourhood is to visit all the households in the area to 'ask for their favour in the future', an application, as it were, for admission to the closed group formed by the local community (although it may well be years before a newcomer is treated as a full member, and even longer before he achieves any real voice in community affairs).

Even such 'modern' institutions as the Parent-Teacher Association of the local school are likely to be a reflection of the patterns of social relations seen in the daily life of the neighbourhood. The PTA chairman will usually be the head of one of the leading families in the community, and the individuals filling other posts will also be found in similar positions in practically every other organisation in the district – the Road Safety Committee, the Old People's Welfare Association, the Crime Prevention Committee, and so on. It is relatively easy to mobilise people and funds for local projects – having street lights installed in the streets of the neighbourhood, for example – but far less easy to do so for schemes which extend beyond the confines of the community. To have a member of the local community active in 'outside' activities – in national politics, for example, or in a senior position in a major company – is desirable not for reasons of local pride (though this does play a part) but because of the advantages that this is likely to bring the community – in the form of a new road, perhaps, or favourable employment opportunities for local children. It is regarded as a natural consequence of membership of the local community that a member should be willing to serve the community in this way. Regional, national, or international issues are of little interest to people except for the impact that they may have on the neighbourhood.

New residential areas

Whilst this description is typical of many of the older residential areas of Japan's cities, it can no longer be regarded as typical of urban life in

An example of the kind of suburban housing that many Japanese aspire to but which, because of the very high price of land, few can afford.

general. The flow of population to the cities in the post-war period has created entirely new residential patterns, ranging from minor 'infilling' of vacant areas in long-established residential areas to whole new towns of several hundred thousand inhabitants built on green-field sites, where all services have to be provided 'from the ground up'. On the whole, however, the new residential areas fall into three fairly distinct groups: the first, which we can call the 'new suburbs', consists mainly of traditional one- and two-storey houses, mostly owner-occupied, extending in an unplanned sprawl around the outskirts of the major conurbations and their satellite towns. The second is a complete break with tradition: large estates – *danchi* – of multi-storey flats, built with public or semi-public funds, and almost entirely rented rather than owned. The third is cheaply-built low-quality housing for rent – the so-called 'Culture Housing' – built to a standard design, and owned by private landlords. The quality of accommodation in these three types of housing differs considerably; so do the residential areas they tend to form.

The 'new suburbs' offer by far the best living environment of the three; built on the edge of the big cities, they are the main contributors to the 'urban sprawl' by which the cities have encroached on the surrounding countryside, engulfing formerly separate towns as they do so. The town where I was recently living is fairly typical. It is some twelve miles north of the main business district of Osaka – Japan's second largest

Left
*One of the vast
estates – Danchi –
of multi-storey
flats in Osaka –
of the kind
referred to in a
recent EEC report
on trade problems
with Japan as
'rabbit hutches'.*

urban centre. Thirty years ago it was a sprawling town with a population of about 20,000 in four separate areas. Mostly agricultural, it even then had a sprinkling of light industry, and housed a certain number of commuters who travelled into Osaka by railway. Ten years ago, when its population had almost exactly doubled, partly by the incorporation of neighbouring villages, it was still regarded as being on the outer limit of the commuter zone, although land prices were steadily rising, and some of the agricultural land nearest to the town centre had been sold for residential development. By the end of 1978 the situation had changed dramatically. The town is now in the *inner* commuter zone, and has a population of over 90,000. There is no scope for further development except on the outskirts of the town, in areas which require a daily return journey of about three hours by bus and train for commuters to the centre of Osaka.

Recent development has nearly all been of large houses – by Japanese standards – and expensive flats for owner occupation, so that the average size of living unit increased by over fifty per cent between 1950 and 1975. It is considerably above the national average, but still means that a family of four have somewhat less space than in a pre-war two-bed-roomed terrace house in Britain. Even allowing for the fact that Japanese living rooms have traditionally done double duty as bedrooms –a pattern that is changing with the introduction of such Western furniture as carpets, beds, and armchairs – and that privacy within the home is less prized than in the West, these standards of space are still very cramped. But the middle-class Japanese is willing to make do with them – even to regard himself as lucky – to commit himself to up to four hours of commuting daily on hopelessly crowded public transport, and to hand

Right
*Tokyo's Central
Station. The
Shinkansen – or
bullet train – is
leaving on the
specially built
tracks at the
right. The other
trains are part of
the vast network
of local railways
which carry more
than 25 million
people a day.*

over perhaps a third of his net salary in mortgage repayments, for the sake of owning a home of his own. In return he is able to live in a neighbourhood which has the potential to develop into a residential community very similar to those in the older urban residential areas, though almost all the new population is made up of commuters and their families, who cannot easily form as close psychological ties with the local community as those who both live and work there.

The *danchi* present a completely different pattern of residential development. Although, like the 'new suburbs', they are built on the outer boundaries, they are estates of multi-storey flats – some of them housing populations of 400,000 or more, and with an average population of perhaps 8,000. They are therefore virtually new towns, but differ from New Towns in Britain because they have been planned from the outset as purely residential areas, with no attempt made to create integrated living and working communities. Over ninety-five per cent of their male population travels to work outside the area where they live. Over five million people – some five per cent of the Japanese population – now live in this kind of accommodation, which is the most rapidly expanding form of residential development. It makes highly intensive use of the available land; the blocks of flats are built oppressively close together, separated only by roads and the occasional tiny childrens' playground. The accommodation they provide is also cramped, with an average of three rooms each of ten feet square or less serving as living and sleeping accommodation for the average family of four. Contrary to the popular impression of austere, sparsely furnished rooms, the average

A young woman's room in the Ogikubo district of Tokyo. Many such rooms are considerably smaller, but just as cluttered.

Japanese home gives the impression of being so crowded with furniture and personal possessions that there is little room for people. I have visited flats in newly-built *danchi* where the only way to store the family's skis was by slinging them from the living-room ceiling!

In favour of most of this sort of accommodation is the fact that, built of reinforced concrete, it is easily heated, secure, and offers a degree of privacy from the neighbours not common in other types of housing. Indeed, one feature of the life-style of the *danchi* residents is what the Japanese refer to as 'my-home-ism'. The *danchi* offer a less favourable environment for the development of a community spirit than almost any other type of residential area. They are large and anonymous, with no natural meeting-place for residents, no local shrine to serve as the focus for the community, and normally no nucleus of 'original inhabitants' around whom such a community could form. In a survey conducted in 1973, an average of sixty-five per cent of *danchi* wives said that the only contact they had with their neighbours was at the level of saying 'good morning' if they met in the street. Only eight per cent said they knew their neighbours well enough to 'participate in outside activities or hobbies with them'. The results of an attitude survey made at the same time indicated that about fifteen per cent of residents wanted to 'assimilate into the local community', and ten per cent had no interest whatsoever in either local or specifically *danchi* affairs. The remaining seventy-five per cent took the attitude that they had the duty and the right to work together – putting pressure on the authorities where necessary – to improve conditions for all. This apparently 'modern' attitude is to some extent deceptive: even in the *danchi* participation in common causes is spasmodic, and only really effective when it closely affects the life of individual families. A recent campaign against a rent increase received massive support in *danchi* throughout the country, but there is little evidence that the same support would be forthcoming for causes which affected individuals less immediately. Community consciousness has been replaced by a stronger awareness of individual rights, but at the moment this shows no signs of growing into anything like a 'social conscience'.

It has been estimated that something like ten per cent of the total population of Japan – over ten million people – lives in the so-called 'Culture Housing' which represents the lowest standard of large-scale housing in Japan today. It accounts for about one-third of the total living units in Metropolitan Tokyo, and a quarter of those in Osaka Prefecture. Located principally in the industrial areas of the larger cities, it consists of one- or two-room flats, often with shared cooking and lavatory facilities, flimsily built of cement and plaster on a wooden framework, expensive to heat, and offering little privacy. The rents are also high, representing on average about one-third of a worker's average take-home pay for a two-room flat. Residents tend to regard themselves as transient – though this is by no means always the case in fact – and have neither the inclination nor the opportunity to develop close links with the local community. They are predominantly recent immigrants to the city, in unskilled and low-paid occupations, with little security of employment, and consequently little hope of obtaining accommodation on more favourable terms. In the absence of an effective policy to control land prices, establish minimum standards of housing, and provide adequate public housing on a massive scale for people in the lower income groups, it is likely that this type of privately-built accommodation – of slum standard from the moment it is built – will continue to represent the best that a large minority of Japan's urban population can aspire to.

A problem common to all kinds of residential area is that the rapid influx of population to the urban areas of Japan has outstripped the capacity of both local government and the public utilities to provide the facilities which in Britain would be taken for granted. The provision of such basic services as main drainage, water, and piped gas, has not only slowed down but in some cases has even been reversed as a result of population pressure. Medical facilities, which are plentiful in the city centres and older residential areas, are extremely sparse in the new commuter zones. Less serious, perhaps, but still important in terms of the overall quality of life, is the generally low level of provision for recreation and culture on anything but a strictly commercial basis. There are few public parks in Japanese cities, and the provision of public libraries ranks so low on the list of priorities that many local authorities have made no provision whatsoever to keep up with population growth.

Above
An increasingly rare sight in Japan today. Rice planting in the evening sunshine in the hills above Kyōto.

Below
A walk in the country. Yukimi Onodera returns home from the Sony factory where she works, for one of her rare visits to her family in the village 200 miles away where she was born and brought up.

Law and Order

It has been a general feature of the industrialisation process throughout the world that urbanisation has been accompanied by an increase in crime. Japan represents perhaps the sole exception, to date, to what has come to be accepted as a virtually universal phenomenon. In Japan's case, despite the extremely rapid growth in urban population since the Second World War, it appears that the crime rate has actually *fallen* over this period from what, in absolute terms, was already a very low level. Generally speaking, such cities as Tokyo and Osaka have less crime – and far less *violent* crime – than cities of comparable size anywhere in the world. Offences against the pornography laws, and so-called 'intellectual offences' such as fraud and forgery, are the only categories to have shown a significant increase over the last twenty years or so. Between 1960 and 1979, for example, the number of murders dropped by nearly twenty per cent, the number of reported cases of rape and assault approximately halved, while there was a sixty per cent drop in the number of reported

The Ginza area of Tokyo at night. Because of the energy crisis many of the lights have now been switched off.

robberies. Even in the seedier entertainment areas of the big cities, full of bars, restaurants, strip shows, and massage parlours, the innocent passer-by is almost entirely safe, apart from the occasional encounter with a drunk. If he goes into one of the less reputable establishments he may well be fleeced, but he is unlikely to be robbed. The causes of this phenomenon are complex, and have yet to be satisfactorily explained, but it seems reasonable to seek a tentative explanation first in the nature of the society and the special features of the urbanisation process, and secondly in the role of the police and their relationship with the general public.

It is generally suggested that the reason for the increase in crime rates as urbanisation proceeds is the breakdown of the tight social organisation that existed in pre-industrial rural society, and which had acted both to inhibit anti-social behaviour and, when such behaviour did occur, to impose its own sanctions rather than rely on legal remedies imposed by the wider society outside the immediate community. It seems that, because of the peculiar course of the industrialisation process in Japan – discussed at the beginning of this chapter – and the way in which the new urban communities were formed, both these features have persisted into contemporary Japan, and have continued to inhibit criminal behaviour. On the formal level each neighbourhood will have its 'Crime Prevention Association', with a weekly rota of 'duty families' to which incidents are reported. The Association is also responsible for contact with the local police, who exercise general guidance over its activities. There are also less obvious sanctions against criminal behaviour; except in the largest and most anonymous *danchi*, everybody in a Japanese residential area knows everybody else and what they are doing, so that the presence of a stranger is soon noticed. If a house is to be left empty, even for an hour or two, the neighbours will be asked to keep an eye on it, and will regard it as a natural part of their neighbourly duty to do so.

The relationships between police and public also fit this general pattern. Each neighbourhood, residential or otherwise, has its own *kōban*, a miniature police station whose duty officers have an intimate knowledge of what is going on in their area. They will call on new arrivals with a questionnaire of such detail that it would be regarded in Britain as a major invasion of privacy, but hardly ever arouses any adverse reaction in Japan. The police go out of their way to involve themselves with the affairs of the neighbourhood, and – with the notable exception of their treatment of left-wing demonstrators – show a remarkable tolerance and willingness to overlook minor misdemeanours, particularly if the culprit is respectful, and shows some sign of remorse.

The courts' approach to the sentencing of convicted criminals reveals a similar attitude. They tend to pay relatively greater attention to the state of mind of the criminal – to the overt signs of repentance or

Above left
*Fuchu Prison. A
group of prisoners
return from
their compulsory
physical education.*

Below left
*Prisoners making
transistor radios.
Work is considered
an essential part
of a prisoner's
rehabilitation.*

Above
*Cells in the block
where prisoners
spend their first
week in solitary
confinement while
their cases are
being assessed.*

otherwise – than to society's need to revenge itself on those who have offended against its norms. As a result, Japanese prisons contain relatively few petty offenders and a correspondingly high proportion of 'hard cases' who have consciously rejected the values of society. The prison system too, while it has its harsh aspects, particularly in the treatment of those regarded as hopeless hardened criminals, places great emphasis on rehabilitation, on enabling the released prisoner once again to become a member of a group, and thus a member of society.

Social welfare

Until the end of the Second World War, such social welfare provisions as existed in Japan were minimal. They were designed for the relief of only the most extreme cases of poverty and distress, and were motivated more by a desire to eliminate possible sources of social unrest, and to avoid possible damage to the health of the population – and therefore to the nation's military and industrial strength – than by a concern for the people's 'welfare' in a humanitarian sense. The traditional attitude in Japan has been that, when an individual falls on hard times, any obligation to assist him lies first with his family, then with his local community – the village in which he lives – and only then, if at all, with higher-level units of administration such as the State. Nor was this attitude – which also existed in the West – modified by a Christian ethic of brotherly love; the ideal of the 'good Samaritan' – that the duty to care for others is general, not restricted to members of any particular group – has remained an alien one, even in modern Japan.

The post-war Japanese Constitution flew in the face of this traditional attitude by laying on the State the duty of striving for the improvement of public welfare and the health of its citizens. It is undeniable that there has been a massive improvement, both in terms of the coverage provided, and the amount of money spent. By the nineteen-seventies Japan could justly claim to have created a comprehensive system of social security, and in the period from 1951 to 1976 the proportion of the national income spent on social security approximately tripled. Since this took place in a period during which the national income was also rising rapidly, it in fact represents a seventeen-fold increase in real terms.

Nevertheless, the Japanese social security system is still beset by problems, both in general policy and in its actual administration. The first and most basic of these is the fact that there still exists no general commitment, at the highest level, to social welfare as a responsibility of the State to all its citizens. The State's role is still basically seen as that of providing a safety net to give protection when all else fails. Generally speaking, therefore, the pattern is one of a mass of private schemes, run by a multiplicity of occupational and other groups – and varying widely in the level of benefits they provide – with a Government-operated scheme providing a much lower level of benefits as a last resort for those not covered by private schemes. Secondly, the persisting attitude that welfare is essentially a concern of the local group to which the individual belongs – combined with the emphasis on community care recently imported from the West – has led the central government to delegate many of its responsibilities in the welfare field to local authorities. It has often neglected, however, to provide them with the financial resources which would enable them to fulfil those responsibilities adequately, and since delegation has often been in the form of enabling rather than mandatory legislation, it has often been ineffective in practice. The great diversity in types of schemes and levels of benefit has thus been exacerbated by wide local differences in the provision both of financial aid and of services. In general the system is complicated and bureaucratic, with the division of responsibility among a large number of public and private agencies, which creates real problems for those trying to administer the system at the 'grass-roots' level, and even more for those who should be its beneficiaries.

Many Japanese are aware of these problems, and considerable progress has been made towards their solution, despite the lack of a common 'philosophy of welfare'. However, there is at present little evidence that the central government is ready to make the commitment to radical change. There are in fact signs that it will attempt to solve its problems by *decreasing* the burden that the system has to carry, rather than by providing the additional resources that are required. The Government is proposing, for example, to raise the age at which old-age pensions become payable from sixty to sixty-five, ostensibly 'to bring the system in line with normal Western practice'. This ignores the fact that the retiring age in Japan, at fifty-five, is some five to ten years earlier than that in most Western countries, and that most Japanese are already obliged to spend ten years after retirement either living off their savings, or taking another job at a drastically reduced salary. It is difficult, in the face of evidence of this sort, to escape the conclusion that there is no real commitment to a 'welfare state' on the part of the Japanese authorities, and that having created a system which at least bears comparison on a superficial level with those of the advanced countries of the West, they feel themselves under little pressure to create a truly comprehensive system of social welfare which would provide for the real needs of the population.

Old age

Old age pensions have already been referred to in the context of the social welfare system, but the whole question of the care of the aged deserves a somewhat wider discussion, if only because of the very high level of awareness of the problem of the aged among the Japanese.

The problem is particularly severe in Japan for a combination of reasons; high and rising standards of medical care have given the Japanese the highest life expectancy in the world and this, combined with the effects of the post war baby boom, and falling birth rates thereafter, has meant that by the year 2020 nearly nineteen per cent of Japan's population will be over the age of sixty-five. At the same time, of course, the relative size of the population of working age, who will have to support the increasing number of old people, is falling proportionately. An increasing financial burden, in other words, will have to be borne by a smaller and smaller number of people. It is on this aspect of the problem that the Japanese Government has concentrated, claiming that the increase in contributions required to achieve the present standards of care means that standards will have to be lowered – notably by raising the age at which old-age pensions are first received, and thus lengthening even further the gap between retiring age and first entitlement to a pension. This approach, with its references to massive increases in contributions by 2020 to retain present levels of pension, is really an attempt to avoid the painful but obvious conclusion that a considerable reallocation of resources will be required. This implies a shift from the insurance principle to a policy of increased support from the national exchequer, no doubt requiring some increase in the general tax burden –

at present one of the lightest in the industrialised world. Until this political decision is taken, with its acceptance of the idea that society as a whole is responsible for the welfare of its older members, expressions of concern by the authorities ring rather hollow.

The problem, however, is not only – or even mainly – a financial one, and as such cannot be solved simply by an increase in Government expenditure. It is part of the whole complex of problems created by Japan's rapid industrialisation and urbanisation and the failure of traditional attitudes and values to keep up with the changes in society.

Traditionally, of course, each family, each village, each local community looked after its own old people who, even when they were no longer capable of productive work, remained as active members of the group, valued for their experience and wisdom, or at least as baby-sitters who could free a younger pair of hands for more productive activities. In 1974, a survey showed that about seventy per cent of Japanese – young people and their older parents alike – thought that the ideal situation was for aged parents to live with their younger children. (In America and West Germany, by contrast, seventy and eighty per cent respectively thought that it was better for them to live apart from their children.) In fact, the proportion of people over sixty-five who *do* live with their adult children, though falling gradually, is still extremely high at over seventy per cent, compared with about forty per cent in the United Kingdom and less than thirty per cent in the United States.

Urbanisation has meant, however, that an increasing number of old people in Japan are faced with the agonising choice between living alone, in the communities they have known all their lives, or uprooting themselves in order to live in the city with their children, whose life-style and values they often no longer share. The latter decision will also often mean a move into considerably more cramped living accommodation, with a resulting reduction in privacy for all members of the family. On the part of the children, too, despite their apparent willingness to conform to the accepted image of the dutiful offspring, there is increasing resentment at the burden – often psychological rather than financial – implied by acceptance of this traditional obligation. (The modern bride's ideal husband is said to be one who has a car, a house of his own and no mother living with him.)

The result has been a considerable increase in the number of old people living alone, as well as in the demand for places in old people's homes, which in recent years have increased quite remarkably in number. The other major achievement has been the rapid strides made towards a thoroughgoing system of medical care for the aged, often at the initiative of progessive local authorities who use their enabling powers to provide services well above the legally-required minimum.

The real problem facing the aged in Japan is often that of loneliness –

The Eijyu-en old people's home in Osaka. Traditional activities like the tea ceremony are very popular with residents who grew up in a very different kind of society.

of coming to terms with a new sort of society and living environment without the support of a traditional community or family. It is in this area that the social services in Japan really fall short. They rely heavily on a system of voluntary visitors (*minsei iin*) which means that help is freely available in the more prosperous residential areas, but almost entirely lacking in the poorer areas and urban slums. The absence of any other charitable tradition in Japan means that old people in these areas, whose need is greatest, are served mainly by a handful of Christian volunteers and dedicated medical workers. Here again the group orientation of Japanese society means that those who are without a group to support them are often left without any support at all.

Marriage and the family

Until the Occupation reforms after the Second World War, the proper relationship between the members of a Japanese family was clearly understood by all concerned; indeed, it was prescribed by law. The Family Law of 1896 gave the father of the family virtually absolute authority over its members, and the Imperial Rescript on Education, which every Japanese child had to learn by heart, also emphasised duty and obedience within the family as one of the main foundations of Japanese society. This was reflected on a national level in the subject's 'filial' duty and obedience to the Emperor. The family was of primary

importance; the individual's interests were regarded as secondary or, rather, were considered as not even existing in isolation from those of the family as a whole.

Within such a social framework it was natural that marriage should be regarded as the concern not of the two individuals involved, but rather of their respective families. Its primary purpose was to provide descendants, and thus to ensure the continuance of the family as a unit. A bride was therefore chosen on the basis of her suitability for child-bearing and rearing, her capacity for hard work, and her adaptability to the ways of the family into which she was marrying, so as to be able to pass on those traditions to the next generation. It was quite common for

Above
Bride and groom at their reception after a country wedding in Kyūshu.

Above right
A smart wedding ceremony in Tokyo.

a marriage not to be registered until she had proved her suitability, particularly by showing that she could produce offspring. She could be divorced at any time if she appeared unsuitable for any reason. The decision for divorce would be taken by the husband's parents; his own feelings were secondary, and this remained so while the husband's parents were alive. His first loyalty was to his father as head of the family; it.was desirable that he should be fond of his wife, but not to such an extent that their relationship interfered with his obligations to the family. The wife's status was often no better than that of a servant, subject to the orders of every member of her husband's family, and particularly to those of his mother. (The popular image of the 'mother-in-law' in Japan is of the *husband's* mother indulging in spiteful bullying of his wife!)

The postwar Constitution and Family Law of Japan established the principle of the equality of the sexes, and of marriage as an institution based on the free consent of both parties. Attitudes to marriage, however, have not changed as quickly as the prescriptions of the law. The proportion of 'arranged' marriages has fallen to less than half of the total, and it is extremely rare for a girl to be forced to accept a partner whom she dislikes, but the status and reputation of the prospective bride's (and, of course, bridegroom's) family are still matters of considerable importance, at least to their parents. A common theme of speeches at weddings in Japan is that the marriage is not simply between two individuals, but between two families. The role of the 'go-between', or sponsor, remains important, even in 'love' marriages, and emphasises the public nature of the marriage relationship as a contract between the families rather than the private concern of the young couple. The parents of a boy or girl of marriageable age will normally ask someone whom they respect and trust to find a suitable partner for their child. Photographs will be exchanged, and a meeting arranged between the couple, with their parents and the sponsor and his wife in attendance. Before this takes place, however, the sponsor will have made extensive equiries into the backgrounds of both families, often using detective agencies which specialise in this type of enquiry. If the couple both agree they will go out together for some time before becoming formally engaged, but it is extremely rare for a couple to agree to meet again with a view to eventually marrying, and subsequently to decide not to go ahead with the marriage. In other words, the commitment to marriage is made, in the great majority of cases, on the basis of a single meeting, in the presence of maybe half-a-dozen other people, where it is likely that the couple will be too embarrassed to exchange more than the most formal of conversations. It is not considered necessary that the couple should know each other well – even less that they should be 'in love' – before committing themselves to marriage. Even if the couple have met independently, fallen in love, and decided to get married, all without the intervention of their parents (as is increasingly the case today), they will normally ask some respectable older couple – the man's section-chief at work and his wife, for example, or their University professor – to act as sponsors, and in this case too the families will usually look carefully into the background of their prospective son – or daughter-in-law. I know a man whose parents opposed his marriage to a girl he had been associating with for over a year because they found that her father was colourblind, and that the marriage would introduce an hereditary weakness into his family line. The man accepted this as a perfectly valid reason for breaking off his engagement.

It is often argued, in favour of the arranged marriage, that the divorce rate is significantly lower than for 'love' marriages. Whilst this is true, the difference is likely to be due mainly to the social pressures against divorce which are applied if an arranged marriage seems to be breaking down. When a marriage is regarded as a contract between two families, then the families – and the sponsors, who are also parties to the contract – are likely to make far greater efforts to keep it going than when it is regarded as the business of the individuals concerned, and of them alone.

In spite of the changes in the law, and of the vast amount of information available in print and on television about what the ideal 'modern' – that is, Western – marriage is like, the contractual nature of marriage also extends to the relations between the husband and wife. In the typical Japanese marriage – far more than is the case in its British counterpart, for example – the partners are seen as having clearly distinguished roles which rarely, if ever, overlap.

The husband's duty is to act as financial provider for the family – his wife, children, and (particularly if he is their eldest son) his parents while they are alive. He is therefore expected to devote himself wholeheartedly to his work, so as to ensure the financial security of the family, both now and after his retirement. At least as far as society is concerned, his performance as a husband is judged almost solely in terms of how well he fulfils these duties; nothing else is required of him.

His wife's job is to run the household, manage the household finances, and bring up the children, a task which includes the supervision of their education. She will not expect her husband to help with the housework or the cooking – even at the weekend – nor to do odd jobs around the house. She should, ideally, get up first in the morning to prepare the family breakfast, and not go to bed until her husband returns from work – or wherever he has been after work, however late he may be. He will not discuss his work with his wife, nor expect her to trouble him with household matters. The only area where their roles overlap to any real extent is where the children are concerned. Although their day-to-day welfare is the wife's job, the husband will be consulted about their education, and be expected to devote some of his free time to them.

Relations between husband and wife will often be affectionate, though the sexual aspect of the relationship is rarely important once the children have been born. They will almost never go out together in the evening, but the man will have ample opportunity for female companionship outside the home, and his wife will be expected to tolerate sexual infidelity on his part, provided that it does not go so far as to threaten the integrity of the family. Infidelity on the part of the wife is not acceptable; it is far more likely to threaten the stability of the home, and as such is a betrayal of her role as wife, mother, and homemaker.

This pattern is typical of wide sections of Japanese society. It could be argued, however, that it is no longer typical of society as a whole, and that young people in particular have far more enlightened, egalitarian attitudes to marriage. In a generation or so, the argument goes, this pattern will be replaced by one which is far nearer to the Western norm. I believe that this argument underestimates the strength with which 'traditional' patterns of behaviour persist in Japanese society, in the face of apparently overwhelming forces. It is true that young people are much freer in their relations with the opposite sex, increasingly choose their own marriage partners without the intervention of their families or sponsors, and enter marriage with a commitment to an equal partnership based on mutual love and respect. This has been true, however, ever since the first generation to have grown up in the post-war period reached marriageable age some fifteen years ago, and the evidence suggests that, in the overwhelming majority of cases, once a couple have been married for a few years, their marriage is far nearer to the 'traditional' pattern than to any 'modern' Western model.

Horrifying though this state of affairs may appear to outsiders with a more egalitarian picture of what marriage *should* be like, or who wish to raise the status of women in society, it may be a perfectly satisfactory situation for the individuals concerned, provided that it satisfies the expectations which *both* of them have for their marriage. In Japan today, although the husband may well be content with this situation, the same is less likely to be true of his wife. She tends to take the idea of an equal partnership more seriously, and would like her husband to take a more active part in the life of the household, rather than assume that his responsibilities are over once his day's work is finished. Whilst she accepts that her husband has duties in his work which keep him away from the family more than is desirable, she would like him to show a little more interest in her and the children. In particular, she is far less likely than in the past to turn a blind eye to his infidelity, regarding it as a real betrayal of the marriage relationship.

There are of course many men who share their wife's view as to what their marriage should be, and make real efforts to create something near to that ideal. It is far more common than in the past for the husband to help out a little in the house – by getting his own breakfast, perhaps, while his wife gets the children ready for school. One even occasionally sees a man – usually young, and looking rather embarrassed – pushing a trolley for his wife as she does the family shopping. It is still practically unthinkable for him to help hang out the family washing – not only because he would think it unmanly, but because his wife would be afraid that the neighbours would regard it as evidence that she was not performing her duties as a housewife satisfactorily. It is difficult, too, to avoid the – perhaps rather cynical – impression that very often the husband's apparent willingness to take part in the affairs of the house is

Three generations of the Onodera family breakfast at home – grand-father (at the head of the table), husband and wife and their three daughters.

no more than a token gesture in the direction of equality. It is a gesture which he may make quite willingly in the early days of the marriage, but which becomes more and more irksome as the relationship becomes routine, and other interests and pressures begin to intrude once more.

Indeed, there is no doubt that the social pressures on the man to conform to the traditional pattern of marriage are very strong, and make it difficult for him to deviate very far. If a man's colleagues are going to a bar after work, for example, he invites ridicule if he excuses himself because his wife is expecting him home for dinner. If he continually makes family obligations an excuse for not joining in the activities of his work-group, he will arouse the suspicion that his loyalty to his family is greater than his loyalty to the group, which could well harm his prospects for promotion in the future. His wife is aware of this danger, and is therefore likely to put up with his late nights, however unhappy she may feel about them.

One area where the behaviour of the typical Japanese husband deviates increasingly from the 'traditional' pattern is in his relationship with his children. He can take his wife for granted, but he is aware that there is little communication between himself and his children, and often tries hard to remedy this deficiency. The gradual move from a six-day to a five-day week is making it easier for him to do this, and an increasing number of office workers are taking a larger part of their holiday entitlement – though very rarely all of it – in order to spend more time with their families. Even so, the typical pattern is still that of a family whose life centres on the mother, with the father as an occasional presence, whose first commitment is to his work and his work-place rather than to his family.

It seems clear from all this that marriage and the family in Japan have not turned into copies of some Western model, but retain features which are still characteristically 'Japanese'. Nor, in my view, is this merely a transitional phase. If anything, the factors working for stability appear far stronger than those working in the direction of further change. There is little evidence that women will make any real effort to raise their own status within the family. The women's movement in Japan is either left-wing and torn by factional discord, or insular and inward-looking. Except for marginal successes in the fields of prices and consumer protection it has achieved little of importance in the last twenty years, and certainly nothing that suggests it is likely to be effective in raising women's consciousness to an extent that could markedly affect the role of women in the family.

On the whole, if the Japanese housewife is frustrated in her expectations of marriage, she appears to resign herself to the situation and turn all her attention and affection towards her children, banking on the next generation, as it were, to provide the fulfilment she has not found in the marriage relationship. One extreme example of this is the phenomenon of the 'education mother', whose whole life appears to be devoted to pushing her children towards ever greater academic efforts. She will stay up until all hours of the night, and even sacrifice holidays with the rest of the family, to provide psychological support for her children in their preparation for examinations. It is by no means unusual to see mothers accompanying their eighteen-year-old sons to the gates of the examination hall when they go to sit the university entrance examinations – in which success should be the reward for all their parental sacrifice. At the same time, Japanese children – boys in particular – are often over-whelmed by their mother with toys and large amounts of pocket-money – and are, as a result, extremely dependent on them.

Outside pressures, too, appear more likely to reinforce the present situation than to bring about further change. Japanese economic success has brought a renewal of confidence in the Japanese way of doing things, and – regardless of whether or not it is an accurate explanation – many Japanese see one of the reasons for that success in the social system in general, and, in particular, in the 'national habit' of selfless hard work and identification by workers with their employer. Since any major change in relationships within the family would require the husband to transfer at least part of his loyalty from firm to family, circumstances seem to be against any real change in the present pattern. This is particularly so at present, when for the first time since the early 1950s there is a real danger of unemployment facing workers in even the largest concerns. Far from transferring their loyalty *away* from their employers, there is if anything an intensification of the competition between employees to show just how loyal they are.

In my opinion, the only event which could bring about a real change in the character of the marriage relationship is a major depression and large-scale unemployment. Given the essentially contractual nature of the relationship, the husband's unemployment, and consequent failure to observe his side of the contract, would almost certainly enable the wife to rewrite the whole contract, as it were, and establish the relationship on a basis more satisfactory to herself. Observation of unemployed workers and their families tends to support this prediction. In the absence of such an economic catastrophe, however, any change in the Japanese family is likely to be gradual, and unlikely to affect the basic pattern of relationships there.

Education

Education is a highly controversial subject in present-day Japan. There is almost universal agreement that a 'crisis in education' exists, but very little about what the problems are, what has caused them, and how they should be solved.

Even before the introduction of a national system of education – based on Western models – in the late nineteenth and early twentieth centuries, the Japanese were keenly aware of the value of education as a means to success in society. The Meiji Government in the late nineteenth century also saw education as a valuable instrument of national policy, and built up a system that was both elitist and meritocratic. The result was the establishment of a small number of institutions of higher education to train the future leaders of the country's Government and industry, combined with a comprehensive system of general and technical education to fit the mass of the population to work in the modern industries which Japan was developing. This essentially 'instrumental' attitude to education – the tendency on the part of both the Government and the population in general to regard it as important because it served a specific useful purpose, rather than as something of value for its own sake – has persisted until the present day. On the one hand this has meant that, as far as the 'consumers' – the parents of the nation's children – are concerned, the quality and content of education are almost irrelevant, provided that it serves its purpose as the passport to a secure, high-status job, while the Government's view of education as an instrument of national policy has led to the creation of a uniform system, subject to strict central control, extending to the minutest details of curriculum and textbook content.

Post-war reforms of the education system created a system which, in principle at least, was thoroughly egalitarian. All children now receive nine years of free compulsory education, starting at the age of six. There has also been a massive increase in the number of high schools and

49

institutions of higher education; more than ninety per cent of the sixteen to eighteen age group are now receiving full-time education, and Japan in 1977 had over four hundred universities, or nearly one thousand if one included all institutions – like Junior Colleges – providing two or more years of full-time education after the age of eighteen.

The system remains, however, highly elitist. There exists a clear hierarchy of prestige among employers, with the most secure – the Civil Service and the largest private companies – at the top of the list. These top employers recruit almost exclusively from a small number of 'top' universities – the older national (public) universities and a few prestigious long-established private institutions. As a result, the competition to enter these top institutions is intense, and the consequence has been the development of a hierarchy among high schools, according to their success-rate in the entrance examinations for the top universities. This process has extended right down the educational scale, with children struggling to pass entrance examinations to the schools which will give

Most kindergartens in Japan are privately owned and fee-paying but, because of the severe pressures of the Japanese educational system, parents are anxious to get their children off to a flying start.

them the best chance of eventually reaching one of the best universities, with its virtual guarantee of a high-status job and security for life. The result is the so-called "examination hell', in which twelve years or more of a child's life are devoted to study for examinations. The social consequences are widespread and tragic.

The most obviously harmful result is what amounts to the sacrifice of the childhood of most of the male (and much of the female) population of Japan for the sake of a university education. A seven-year-old just starting school can expect an average of perhaps an hour's homework a night, rising to two hours or more by the time he is eleven and the entrance examinations for middle school are only two years away. Many children have extra classes after school; my eleven-year-old son was the only boy in his class of forty at the local Japanese junior school who was not attending a 'cramming-school' on at least one night a week! Enlightened teachers are virtually helpless in the face of parental pressure for ever more homework so that their children do not fall behind in the academic rat-race.

Official Government policy is to provide 'education suited to the abilities of the individual', but this conflicts directly with the same government's obsession with uniformity, and parents' fears that their own children are not getting the same opportunities as others. The Ministry of Education has if anything exacerbated the situation by progressively lowering the age at which various sections of the curriculum are taught, thus increasing the quantity of information that has to be absorbed by a child at any stage in his school career. Many children are thus under a double stain: they are subjected to a heavy and increasing load of school work, and those who fall below the highest standards are branded as failures, in the eyes of both society and their own parents. In recent years there has been a disturbing increase in the number of child suicides, with younger children increasingly involved. In 1977 there were 784 cases of suicide by persons under twenty years of age – itself a considerable increase on the previous year; the figure for 1978 was 886, representing an increase of at least twelve per cent over the figure for 1977, and in the first quarter of 1979 at least a hundred children and young people committed suicide every month. Judging from the notes left by these children, the two most common factors pushing them to suicide appear to be worries about schoolwork or examinations, and unhappiness at home. In fact, these two factors often appear together. Instead of being able to turn to his parents for sympathy when things are not going right at school, a child all too often finds that his mother – since his father is rarely available – takes an even fiercer attitude than the school authorities, and simply urges him to further efforts. That suicides by children still in primary school – that is, under the age of thirteen – have suddenly increased is surely no more than a reflection of the shift of the pressure of the examination system lower and lower down the age scale, and of the inadequacy of the contemporary Japanese family to cope with the results of this pressure. In this sense, the problem of child suicides is part of a whole complex of problems, and is unlikely to be solved in isolation.

The situation would be less tragic if the examinations for which the child spends most of his life preparing were designed to test the real intellectual ability of the candidates. In fact they are almost exclusively tests of memory, requiring candidates to regurgitate facts and formulae learnt by heart, regardless of whether or not they have been understood. Much of the teaching directed towards these examinations is therefore a complete waste of time in any other context, particularly in such fields as history, literature, and foreign languages. The poor performance of the Japanese in English is a good example; it is difficult to find a university graduate who can carry on even a rudimentary conversation in the language, even though he must have studied it for at least ten years. The reason is that English as studied for examination purposes bears little relation to the language as it is spoken in England or North America, and a similar situation applies, to a greater or lesser extent, in the majority of other subjects.

The eagerness to obtain entrance to a top-ranking university is such that, having invested twelve years of their lives, thousands of students are willing, having failed the examinations the first time round, to spend another one, two, or more years attending 'preparatory schools' – profit-making (and highly profitable) institutions whose sole purpose is to prepare first-time failures for their second and subsequent attempts. The majority of candidates who fail at their first attempt for a place at a top university, however, will have also taken the examinations for others, less prestigious – and therefore easier to enter. Other students with less confidence in their ability will have attempted one university of the second rank, perhaps, with two or three of the third or fourth rank as 'insurance'. It is possible for any student who has graduated from high school to obtain a place at a university if his parents are willing both to pay for it, and to accept what is often a university education in name only. The majority of private universities rely almost entirely on student fees for their income, with inevitably harmful effects on the quality of teaching. A ratio of students to teachers of fifty to one or higher is commonplace (compared with something like twelve to one in the best public universities), and personal contact between staff and students is virtually impossible. The universities themselves have in many cases accepted their role as mere degree factories; several have no lecture halls capable of accommodating anything like the number of students who should be attending lectures. Nor do the students demand anything better; in the majority of cases they are at the university to obtain not an

A Kendo class, one of many popular out of school activities. 'Kendo', says one master, 'is not a means of violence, but a way of forming a sound mind and a sound body.

education but a graduation certificate, and welcome four years of freedom between the twelve-year examination treadmill and a lifetime in a job which is unlikely to fulfil their earlier expectations.

For a degree from such a 'degree factory' will not, of course, secure a job in one of the 'top' firms. So many university graduates come on to the job market each year that many of them are obliged to accept posts that in Britain would be filled by sixteen-year-olds with two or three CSE passes. (As an example, every one of the delivery boys for the Co-operative Society in the district where I was recently living had a university degree!) Many students realise this even before leaving high school, but enter university nevertheless, feeling that any university degree is better than none at all.

The pressures of the examination system relax almost completely once the hurdle of university entrance is passed. Japanese universities are difficult to enter, but very easy to graduate from; attendance at enough lectures to enable him to amass the required number of 'credits', and a token performance in the final examination, will be enough for a student to obtain a degree from all but the most scrupulous of univers-

A language laboratory. Though schools put a lot of effort into teaching English, few Japanese seem able to carry on a coherent conversation in the language.

ities. Many students do of course devote themselves to serious study, but there is little pressure to do so, and the great majority seem content to enjoy the breathing space which their student days offer them.

A minority of students, however, have reacted to the situation not with resignation but with apparently mindless violence. Given a Marxist view of society – which is far more widespread in Japan than in Britain or the United States – it is not surprising that some students should look back on their years of intensive study, and forward to an even longer period of possibly unrewarding work, and see in their own experience a typical example of the sacrifice of human values to serve the needs of capitalist society. Nor do they see any real evidence that the universities and their staff – with a few notable exceptions – are particularly interested in the real problems of society, or, for that matter, in the welfare of their students. Since the established political parties and the democratic process have had conspicuously little success in reforming the system, the only solution appeared to be its destruction. The result was a wave of violence which swept through the universities throughout Japan in the late 1960s and early 1970s. It was led by a small minority of left-wing militants, but the rapid spread and nationwide scale of the disturbances would not have been possible had these extremists not gained the sympathy and at least tacit support of a far larger number of moderates, who shared their anger and frustration with the system, if not their ultimate objectives. Only when it became clear to the moderate majority that the militants were interested not in the reform of the system, but its destruction, and were engaging in violence for its own sake rather than as a rational means to an end, did the violence subside. Even today a few of the most militant splinter groups are still engaging in what amounts to sporadic guerilla warfare, though they have almost completely lost the sympathy of the main body of students.

These upheavals stimulated the production of a host of plans for reform of the system, some of which have been put into effect. The Ministry of Education, for example, has created a new university at Tsukuba, in the country north of Tokyo, by transferring there one of Tokyo's long-established and reputable national universities. Tsukuba – heralded as the university of the future – has a new administrative structure, under far tighter Ministry control than other national universities, and seems to be trying to solve the problem of student unrest by moving the university away from the disturbing influence of society, and by suppressing any sort of student activity which has anti-establishment aims or overtones. Rather than try to remove, or at least alleviate, the very real causes of student frustration, the Ministry is content simply to suppress its outward manifestations.

Other solutions – reform of the entrance examination system for the public universities, for example, and increased Government subsidies for the private sector – are being tried, but they are partial at best, and often tailored to the demands of particular political prejudices and vested interests. The national universities resist anything which threatens their privileged position; the private sector is also jealous of its freedom, and even though it is in financial difficulties, is also afraid of the interference which might accompany Government aid. Government and industrial circles tend to regard the whole problem as evidence of the corruption of society by left-wing ideas implanted by Marxist teachers, while the Left sees it as the natural result of the policies of a reactionary Government which has used education to serve the interests of the capitalist system. The whole problem is bedevilled by the fact that there no longer exists a consensus, amongst the population as a whole, about what the root causes of the problem are, or even about what the role of education in contemporary Japan should be.

Until relatively recently some such consensus did exist. Economic expansion was a common national goal, shared by almost all sections of the population, and the role of education was to assist in achieving that goal. Although to the outside observer this may seem an appallingly narrow definition, it fits the predominantly 'instrumental' way of thinking of the Japanese, in which institutions – including education – are judged by their effectiveness as a means to specific ends, rather than as important for their own sake. Judged in that light the achievements of the education system in Japan have been considerable. Despite the formidable obstacles posed by the uniquely complicated Japanese writing system illiteracy is virtually non-existent, and the education system

has undeniably played a valuable role, first in assisting Japan to industrialise faster than any of her predecessors, and then, after the Second World War, to achieve a rate of economic growth unsurpassed in the West. It is only recently, as the Japanese themselves have started to question the suitability of economic development as an overriding objective, that they have also begun to wonder whether the benefits of their educational system, which has served them well so far, may not now be outweighed by its harmful effects. An increasing number of parents are trying to get their children into the junior and middle schools attached to many of the private universities, which virtually guarantee eventual entrance to that university without subjecting the student to a succession of entrance examinations. Study abroad is another increasingly popular escape route. It is relatively easy to obtain entrance to a university abroad, and the demand for foreign-language speakers in Japan is such that a graduate of, say, a third-rate American university who can speak English fluently stands a far better chance of obtaining a good job than would one from a Japanese university of similar standing. Finally, there appears to be a growing number of parents who are willing for their children not to go to university at all if they do not seem particularly gifted academically. The growth of unemployment, even among university graduates, strikes at the whole basis of a system in which a university education has been regarded as a passport to the security of lifetime employment. If Japan

A school visit to the Heian Shrine in Kyōto. In a country where few families take holidays together, such educational visits may well be the only chance a child has to travel away from home during schooldays.

56

has indeed entered a new phase of slow growth and persistent unemployment – even at levels which are low by British standards – it is conceivable that what is at the moment a barely discernible trend may turn into a full-scale reaction against the present system of university education. This might then lead to a serious search for a new consensus about the role of education in society. Without this, a real solution of the 'crisis' in Japanese education is unlikely to be achieved.

The future

It will be clear from what has gone before that I do not believe that Japan is in the process of turning into some sort of Asian version of the 'advanced' countries of the West, different from them only in superficial details. It is therefore all the more difficult to attempt any sort of forecast as to how Japanese society *will* develop in the future.

On the one hand, the society has shown over the last century a remarkable capacity to absorb what have appeared to be irresistible pressures for change with remarkably little effect on its basic structure. There is little evidence to suggest that the situation is going to change in the immediate future. The economic success of the post-war years has given the Japanese a renewed sense of confidence in what they see as the Japanese way of doing things. Even the turmoil and disillusionment caused by Japan's defeat in 1945 did not cause a major shift in attitudes and behaviour patterns; it is unlikely that the present mood of self-confidence and pride in Japan's achievements will do so. Whilst the Japanese are well aware of the problems facing their society, they no longer feel impelled to look to the West for solutions, as they have in the past. Both Western individualism and various versions of Marxism have their adherents in considerable numbers, but have had little impact on attitudes in society as a whole. The (somewhat distorted) picture that most Japanese have of the outside world does not give them the impression that Britain, say, or the Soviet Union have any fewer problems than they themselves face. Any solution to these problems therefore is likely to be found within the framework of the present structure of Japanese society.

This does not imply, however, that change will not take place, nor even that it will necessarily be gradual when it does occur. The structure of Japanese society – a set of closed groups, each absorbed in the pursuit of its own objectives to the virtual exclusion of wider interests – certainly makes it highly resistant to any change which would conflict with those objectives. But Japanese society is also characterised by very high degree of uniformity – both racial and cultural – which manifests itself on one level in a general inclination to follow the latest fashion, in sport, entertainment, clothing or the choice of a destination for a trip abroad.

It is also present, however, on the level of attitudes and objectives; the competing groups of which the society is composed are often virtually indistinguishable to the outside observer. (A 'Mitsui man' and a 'Mitsubishi man' are cast in the same mould, as it were; only the labels are different.) This feature of the society means that it is capable of making very dramatic changes of direction. All that is required is that a directive from the leadership of the group should be passed down from the top. Providing that it fits the prevailing 'mood' – which will have been created, or at least sensed, by the leadership before the decision is taken – a new group objective is relatively easily established. Given the uniformity of the society, a new set of *national* objectives can be set up through a similar process of 'mood-creation' on a national scale, followed by a political decision at the highest level, which has the appearance of having been taken in response to popular demand. This may in fact be the case, of course, but it is not really important how the consensus arises; what does matter is that it exists, and that the decision to act is taken from above, and passed down as 'group policy'.

It is this that has led me to emphasise the importance of national consensus, or its absence, where such topics as the reform of the education system are concerned. On that particular topic it appears that a mood is developing in favour of some sort of reform; it is too early to say whether it will become strong enough to stimulate a radical change of policy. Much the same is true of the other problems that Japan faces. All that can safely be said is that in spite of – or, paradoxically, as a result of – the persistence of 'traditional' patterns of social organisation, she is more likely to attempt radical solutions, and to put them into effect, than is the case in supposedly more 'modern' countries like Britain and the United States.

2
The changing attitudes of young people
Richard Boyd

Introduction

For some years now commentators have discussed the rapid social changes which have occurred in Japan since the Second World War as the result of the development of what they call a post-industrial society. Briefly, they argue that these changes are symptomatic of a crisis which is common to most advanced industrial nations. Such societies are at a point of transition from economies in which most of the labour force works in manufacturing industry to economies in which services – like finance, insurance, commerce, and property – are dominant. The implications are enormous. Whereas unskilled manual workers were the basic productive force of the industrial society, it is the skilled, the educated, the 'technocrats' who are now the most important group. It is in their image, and to meet their needs, that the new post-industrial society will be shaped. The United States, they argue, is in the first stages of this development. Japan is heading in the same direction and following close behind.

Now there is no denying that, as a consequence of a significant increase in personal income, the existence of a vigorous private enterprise system, the absence of restraints – like religion or a strong state – on changing tastes, the *outward* appearance of the life of the Japanese people has been transformed – seemingly overnight. But it is much more difficult to assess quite how thoroughgoing the transformation has been. We need to know the answer to the question asked by Professor Watanuki in his recent book, *Politics in Post War Japanese Society*, 'What of the inner life', he asks, 'the world of the mind where values reign? Have the great changes in the Japanese economy exerted a similarly strong impact on this realm as well? Does a young Japanese man in his colourful shirt and wide tie or a young Japanese woman in her mini skirt and leather boots think at all like an American or West European youth with similar consumer tastes? Or underneath these new styles does the young Japanese still share the values of the older generation?'

The post-industrial society theory assumes that the changes are not superficial, that new patterns of consumption have been accompanied by the spread of new values more appropriate to this new style of life and that, as a result, a gap has opened up between the generations, 'the young being readier than the old to accept both the new style and the new values associated with it'. It is this assumption that I want to examine a little more closely. But first a note of caution. If it does appear that new, deep-rooted values have emerged, these are not necessarily evidence of the transition from an industrial to a post-industrial society. Similarly, if there is evidence of a generation gap, it should not be assumed that this is necessarily the same thing as a clash between traditional and post-industrial values.

'Outward' changes in Japanese society

The 'outward' changes in the appearance, leisure pursuits and consumption patterns of people in Japan have to be seen in the context of the massive growth of the Japanese economy in the last twenty-five years. Gross National Product increased from £14,000 million in 1955 to £290,000 million in 1975 – ten times greater than the growth in population. This vast increase in personal wealth has had a great impact on consumption right across the board, but one of the most significant consequences has been the creation of an enormous market for consumer goods amongst younger people.

Traditionally, the Japanese employment system distributed rewards (in the form of wages and promotion) on the basis of seniority. This meant that young people (men in the eighteen to twenty-seven and women in the eighteen to twenty-five age groups) had an average wage considerably lower than that of their seniors and, as a consequence, less purchasing power. The tendency for the benefits of increased productivity to filter down through the pyramid of the employment system meant that young peoples' wages would in any case have benefited from economic expansion, but this process was accelerated by the boom in labour intensive industries such as construction. This, in turn, led to a labour shortage and the resulting competition for newcomers to the labour market (primarily the young) led to a significant rise in the wages paid to the young. Since at the same time there was an enormous increase in the opportunities for part-time employment, even those young people who were still being educated could earn substantial amounts of pocket money. Many of these young people live at home with their parents.

*'Let's Go Young',
a regular Sunday
evening television
pop programme,
which shows
the overwhelming
influence of western
styles and images.*

They do not have heavy commitments – no mortgages to pay off, no children to educate, no medical expenses to pay, no retirement to provide for. Apart from a nominal contribution to household expenses their net income is therefore also their disposable income, and for some young people this can now be as much as £500 a month.

Business was not slow to appreciate the importance of a market of over fifteen million young people with this kind of money to spend. A sophisticated and extremely influential advertising industry trains its

guns on the young through six commercial television channels and a multitude of pulp magazines, 'fanzines' and comics, and rarely misses the target. The fascination of young Japanese with the West and with Western fashions is exploited unmercifully. Ironically, the persistence of a traditionally Japanese phenomenon, the overriding importance of the group – the primacy of group identity over individual or self-identity – makes young people extraordinarily vulnerable to rapid changes of fashion. This guarantees that that which has to be bought today will be obsolete tomorrow, when something equally essential will take its place. Once the group has latched on to a new fashion *everyone* in the group must acquire it or declare themselves outside the group. The speed and comprehensiveness of these changes are staggering: mini skirts are replaced by maxi skirts, A lines by H lines, the 'Ivy League' look by the 'Cool and Free' West Coast look. American films play a crucial part in the process – *Saturday Night Fever*, for example, was given huge publicity and became enormously popular before anyone had even seen the film. The clothing industry produced white suits and black shirts by the thousand, the department stores bought the sound-track record in bulk and the manufacturers of audio equipment anticipated with relish another new stimulus to their trade. At last the film broke – first in Tokyo but soon after in all the cities – and overnight Japan was populated by John Travolta and Olivia Newton John look-alikes. The discotheques

Above
Saturday Night Fever sweeps Japan. Aspiring John Travoltas display themselves on a Sunday afternoon in the Harajuku district of Tokyo.

Right
A group of fashionably dressed young women keeping an eye on the latest trends.

Above and below
*Young people in
Japan have plenty
of money to spend.
It is they who
buy most of the
consumer durables
and who are most
receptive to new
ideas, especially
from the West.*

were full of people doing the new dances (for that matter the parks were full of people *practising* the new dances, so seriously is fashion treated in Japan). Meanwhile the clothing industry, the record trade, the stores and boutiques were preparing for tomorrow's craze.

It would be wrong to present all such Western imports in terms of a cynical 'ad-mass' manipulation. Many of the 'new' leisure pursuits and consumer preferences have established themselves firmly in the Japanese culture. Young people eat less rice and more bread, meat, eggs, and fruit. They drink coffee in preference to green tea, and beer, coke, and whisky and water in preference to sake. In the cities 'Macdonalds', 'Kentucky Fried Chicken', and 'Mr Doughnut' compete with the noodle shop and the barbecued chicken stands; bowling alleys have come and gone, but

Above
Sumo wrestlers at the Spring Festival of the Yasukuni Shrine in Tokyo.

Below
Japan's oldest professional base-ball team, the Yomiuri Giants, practise at the Korakuen Stadium in Tokyo for the start of the new season.

weekend ski resorts have persisted; and baseball and golf rival sumo wrestling as the national sport.

It must not be assumed either that such borrowing is a one-way process. Japanese interest in Western arts has provided a stimulus, and above all a financial support, that the West could not provide. This is particularly true of Western music. Japan is the second largest record market in the world (it accounts for eleven per cent of global sales per annum) and has an insatiable appetite for eighteenth and nineteenth century music, for traditional and modern jazz, for pop, for hard rock and country rock, and latterly for 'New Wave' and 'Tex-Mex' music. In addition to the normal channels (radio, television, concert halls, etc.), Japan's myriad coffee shops provide a highly specialised outlet for

Western music. Some play only classical music, others 'Singer-Song Writers', 'fusion', jazz rock and 'cross-over'. In some establishments the music provides a backdrop for coffee and conversation, in others the coffee gets cold and conversation is frowned on (unless of course it concerns Ben Webster's vibrato, Max Roach's brush work or Glenn Gould's tempi).

So deeply rooted are Western musical idioms that the young Japanese is now more likely to take up the violin, guitar, or piano than traditional instruments like the koto or shakuhachi. Young performers of classical, jazz, and rock music have acquired international reputations and, more recently, young composers working in Western idioms have emerged. It might be added that although the domestic popular music founded on a rich folk tradition remains in favour with the young in Japan, 'classical' Japanese music does not. Indeed it can be said to suffer from woeful neglect.

Scenes in Kyōto – a city dominated by Buddhism.

Above
Patterns on the gravel at Tofukuji.

Below
The Moss Garden at Saihōji.

Youth and Politics

A thorough-going transformation – some would say 'Westernisation' of the appearance, leisure pursuits, and consumption of the young has undoubtedly occurred. These changes, even the seemingly superficial ones, have important consequences for the society as a whole, for the older generation as much as the younger. The preference of the young for bread, for example, has greatly reduced the demand for rice, which poses a threat to the livelihood of Japan's rice farmers. The rice farmers have been among the major supporters of the ruling Liberal Democratic Party. If the numerical and strategic significance of groups such as the rice farmers continues to decline, the LDP will be faced both with the problem of re-establishing its social base and with the prospect of electoral defeat.

Although therefore it would seem that even changes in consumption can have important social and political repercussions, it has been argued that 'older generations' of Japanese have attempted to control the flow of imports from the West and to filter out those ideas, principles, and practices that seem to present an obvious and direct threat to the existing social and political organisation of Japan. In short, it is fine for Japanese youth to wear outrageous Western fashions and to let off steam at rock concerts, provided that at the appropriate time they accept the rigorous group discipline of the firm and subscribe to the dominant values of the social and political consensus. In this perspective, the country's success in filtering out what are perceived as less desirable Western values is a partial explanation of (and is confirmed by) the high degree of consensus and the low level of conflict in Japan. This is underlined by such factors as governmental stability, the insignificance of political opposition, the

Above
View from
the verandah at
Shisendo in Kyōto.

Below
In the garden
at Shisendo.

relative tranquillity of industrial relations, the low crime rate and the low divorce rate.

This view is unacceptable to prophets of the post-industrial society, who have assumed from the first that the transition to post-industrialism has inevitable consequences for politics as well as for society. In particular, they have argued that, sooner rather than later, the Liberal Democratic Party, supported as it has been for twenty-five years by tradition-orien-tated groups – farmers, fishermen, merchants, small manufacturers, the less well-educated, and older people – would be voted out, and a new and powerful coalition of socialist-led reformist forces from the modern sectors of the population – white collar workers, manual workers, the more highly educated and the young – would come to power. Unfor-tunately for the theory, Japan enters the 1980s with the Liberal Demo-crats more securely entrenched than they have been for a decade. Rather than rely on simple theoretical formulae, it would be better to look at the actual *experience* of, and attitudes to, politics, work, education, marriage, sexual morality, and crime, and decide for ourselves if there is any evidence of changing values in these areas.

To begin with, there is little evidence for the idea that Japanese youth is apathetic and apolitical. There is, however, much truth in the view that young people reject certain kinds of formal political institutions and prefer an individual and participatory style of politics. In particular, they have very little confidence in their political leaders. The Emperor is seen as a figure of little significance, while the Prime Minister is felt to be 'unlikeable and untrustworthy'. The difference between the attitudes of the young and of their parents to Japan's political leaders is marked as early as the age of thirteen. And yet the cynicism with which political leaders are regarded is not part of a generalised cynicism about political life as a whole. While the young place little reliance upon their leaders they have much more positive feelings about elections, parties, and popular participation in politics than the older generation. One com-mentator suggests that 'this constitutes a major redirection of Japanese political culture, away from one in which the prevailing pattern was for the individual to relate to politics mainly or exclusively as a subject, oriented primarily toward the authorities, to a pattern in which the individual perceives politics as a process in which he has a stake and a voice, and a right to have that voice heard'.

And yet the importance that the young attach to participation is no guarantee of the vitality of formal political institutions. Indeed, the reverse is closer to the truth, since it seems that the intensification of the desire to participate is often related to a growing distrust of the institu-tionalised channels of participation – elections and political parties. An-other consequence of the enthusiasm for participation therefore is 'the decline of political parties and the rise of various voluntary citizens and residents movements which dislike, and refuse to follow the leadership of, any political party and prefer protests to institutionalised participation'. In this respect it is significant that, in a recent survey, seventy per cent of those under twenty and fifty per cent of those between twenty and thirty claimed that they supported no political party. The political behaviour of the young reflects these attitudes. More people in the twenty to twenty-nine age group than in any other age group do not vote in elections. Moreover, the rate of abstention for young people has increased steadily in the last twenty years. This failure to vote is combined with relatively high support for the 'progressive' opposition parties and low support for the ruling Liberal Democrats. Nearly forty per cent of the twenty to twenty-nine age group support the opposition (the largest proportion of any age group) while only twenty-two per cent support the LDP (the lowest proportion of any age group).

The contradiction between their eagerness to participate and their distrust of political parties is not lost on the young. It leads them to doubt their own political system and to wonder if Japanese democracy is quite what it should be. The author is, presumably, not the first visiting Western political scientist who has learnt to deny his calling; to claim to be a sales representative rather than answer the question which follows inevitably upon confessing an interest in Japanese politics to young people: 'What do you *really* think of Japanese democracy?' It is not enough to stone-wall, to counter with doubts about one's own country – the virulence of the 'English disease', the loss of confidence in familiar institutions which has followed our seemingly ineluctable industrial decline. Indeed it comes as a surprise, though a pleasant one, to hear that these questions are irrelevant, that the greatness of Britain is guaranteed by its 'defeat of fascism' and its 'gift to the world of parliamentary government'. One such conversation – the consequence of an ill-advised failure to take the sales representative option – springs to mind; in the course of this a young salary man loudly insisted that the Japanese people would never again tolerate the militaristic adventures of their leaders 'because now we are a democracy', only to insist with equal vigour a few moments later that the major political parties are 'no good', that they are 'as bad as each other' and not concerned with 'the right questions'.

The dissatisfaction of the young with formal channels of participation has not yet had serious consequences for the political system. Its potential significance has, however, been much increased since the crisis of 1973 by the bleak employment situation which increasingly faces young people, and particularly university graduates (who are even less satisfied with politics, and more prone to abstain, than others in their age group). Though Japan has certainly shaken off some of the worst effects of the 1973 oil crisis, the massive growth rate of the 1960s seems now to be a thing of the past. Leading firms are reluctant to recruit large numbers of

One of the demonstrations against the opening of the new Tokyo airport in the spring of 1978.

graduates when the prospects for expansion are so poor. Such is the climate of uncertainty indeed that when the economy began to recover in 1978 Japanese firms preferred to recruit women (as they could be dismissed more easily should there be a downturn) and to offer part-time rather than full-time employment.

In spite of these new economic realities the number of graduates with high expectations about the kind of work appropriate to their station increases every year. The intensity of competition for the limited number of positions in business, central and local government increases accordingly. Between 1973 and 1978, for example, the ratio of job offers to applicants in the twenty to twenty-four age group fell by a half, and for nineteen-year-olds even more sharply. Many of these young people will be disappointed and will be faced with the painful necessity of lowering their expectations. If they are not prepared to do this there may well, in the long term, be serious political problems.

It is at least conceivable that those problems will include a recrudescence in the 1980s of violent political action by young radicals of the left and right similar to that of the mid 1970s. Some of these groups, such as the notorious Sekigun (Red Army Faction), have virtually disappeared, but other Marxist-Leninist factions (such as *Kakamaruha* and *Chukakuha*) remain important. They are committed to violent revolution and – as was confirmed by the mass demonstrations and violent clashes with the police at the opening of Narita Airport in 1978 – they are still capable of mobilising thousands of supporters. Activists committed to violent revolution are a minority of perhaps thirty to forty thousand

71

young Japanese. Ideologically they are very different from the majority, for whom 'peace stands at the pinnacle of the hierarchy of social values'. Moreover, the young are the staunchest of all age groups in their defence of the democratic constitution.

The peaceful majority, however, includes an important, non-violent, activist element which was radicalised by the troubles surrounding the ratification of the United States–Japan Security Treaty in 1960 and 1970. A popular myth has it that these young people are radical at twenty and a bastion of the 'establishment' in business and government at forty. This is not in fact the case. One follow-up study of the 'Ampo generation' – which opposed the 1960 Treaty – reveals that while former activists do not become professional revolutionaries after graduation, neither do they strive for access to the commanding heights of economic and political power. The majority enters the professions, particularly the 'intellectual' professions of teaching, journalism, and publishing, and not industry, commerce, and the Civil Service. Many of these activists planned to combine political activity with their chosen occupation and hoped to work to change the capitalist system after they graduated. All this, concludes the study, 'indicates that the students, particularly the activists who wished to, and did, enter the professions, were seeking an

November 1960 – one of the mass demonstrations against the Treaty of Mutual Co-operation and Security with the United States.

occupational environment that would allow them to fulfil their personal political values'. The study's findings also suggest that the activists' beliefs do not change as they get older. They remain leftist, politically alienated, but eager to make their views known.

Many radicals have found a congenial working environment in higher education. Élite universities like Tokyo, Kyoto, and Keio number former leaders of *Zengakuren*, the Communist-led broad front of student unions, among their teaching staff. Some have been content to 'humanise' staff-student relations, channelling their radicalism into a generalised concern for the students quite out of keeping with the tradition of rigid, impersonal master-disciple relations common to much of higher education in Japan. Others, such as the 'progressive teachers' in Kyoto and Tokyo Education University, and in Tokyo University itself, have been much more self-assertive. They have advised, guided and even led student protest movements and organised opposition to attempts to rusticate student militants because, as a distinguished radical professor at Hiroshima University has put it, 'the distance between the university and the people is short, but the distance between the government and the people is long'.

It is perhaps the memories of the Ampo struggle that colour young peoples' attitudes to the USA. There is a strong tendency amongst young Japanese to reject the USA in favour of Western Europe; this distinguishes them from the older generations who lived through the war, and yet are more likely to like the USA. Indeed, a recent survey found that those under nineteen dislike the USA more than the USSR, while as many twenty to twenty-four-year-olds disliked the USA as much as the USSR – whereas older people are overwhelmingly hostile to the Soviet Union. It should, however, be pointed out that a large number of young people neither disliked nor felt threatened by any country.

Youth and Work

The official school leaving age is fifteen but over ninety per cent of pupils carry on with their studies and graduate from high school at eighteen. The majority of these high school graduates enter the labour market and find employment. A substantial minority, however, now continue their education after the age of eighteen. The expansion of higher education over the last twenty years has indeed been truly remarkable. In 1955 only one in ten high school pupils went on to university or college; in 1980 the figure is rather better than one in three and Japan has a student population in excess of two million.

The eagerness of the young to acquire educational qualifications is a rational response to a society which insists on translating the ability of an individual directly, and simply, in terms of his educational qualifica-

Yasuda Hall, Tokyo University - the apex of the Japanese education al hierarchy.

tions. The key qualification is a university degree. As one authority has pointed out, 'a man with only qualifications up to high school level, *whatever his ability and experience*, cannot compete with a university graduate in obtaining employment or in climbing the promotion ladder'. In addition to this clear distinction between university graduates and high school leavers there is a rigid ranking order among schools and universities, which is most rigid at university level. The rank of the university determines the life chances of an individual. It opens up some positions of status and prospects of success and forecloses others. The most prestigious firms recruit from the most prestigious universities. The apex of the university pyramid is the University of Tokyo; graduation from Tokyo unites and binds students almost regardless of their regional or socio-economic background and constitutes a passport to elite positions in business and government. In 1974, for example, graduates of this university held 141 of the 169 top positions in the Civil Service and, of the 303 biggest firms in Japan, 124 were presided over by Tokyo University graduates. Political parties, including the Communist Party, are also controlled by the graduates of Tokyo University.

For the less well qualified, the major opportunities have been in the rapidly expanding services sector, which now employs more than half of the working population. As early as 1960, for example, the young accounted for fifty-three per cent of all clerks in Japan. In short, Japan is well on the way to becoming a white collar society and the white collar worker in large business enterprises or governmental departments, known as a 'salary man', has become the target occupation for many young people.

A young man – particularly a graduate – enters his firm in the certainty that this will be his work place until retirement at fifty-five. The pressure on him to adjust his values to those of his colleagues is consequently very strong; an adjustment which is likely to favour traditional values since the workforce still contains a large proportion of older workers who are committed to the values of hard work and loyalty to their company and who accept the predominantly paternalistic Japanese management style. The pressures to conform to these traditional values are reinforced by a refocusing of the young worker's social life after he joins the company. This is now centred on a group of colleagues from one department or section who not only work together but also eat and drink together in local bars and restaurants after work. So strong are these pressures that, if he is married, the young man distances himself more and more from his family, effective responsibility for which devolves upon his wife.

The younger generation in Japan, in comparison with the previous, older generation is, however, less work-orientated, less organisation-orientated and more self-assertive. There is already, and there is bound in the future to be more, stress on individual ability and performance and on greater democracy at work. And yet it would be unwise to exaggerate the likely dimensions of the change. Rather more than the youth of America, France, and Britain, young Japanese define themselves in terms of their job, and see the opportunity of realising themselves as fully-developed individuals in their work as being the most important thing in their lives. It is perhaps significant, however, that a young Japanese worker can ask his English language teacher if there is an English equivalent of 'Blue Monday' – the depression at the beginning of the working week that is widely felt by Japanese workers.

Young women in Japan: changing attitudes

The figures for high school pupils proceeding to colleges and universities suggest that male and female students have roughly equal chances of a place in higher education. But whereas (in the most recent survey) forty-three per cent of eligible males carried on with their studies, only thirty-two per cent of eligible females did so. Moreover, the majority of young women entered the relatively low-status Junior colleges, where about ninety per cent of the students are women, while the membership of the universities in general, and the élite high status establishments in particular, is overwhelmingly male. Since, as we have seen, the positions of greatest prestige and status are reserved for graduates of the universities with the greatest prestige and highest status, the substantial exclusion of women from the universities ensures their exclusion from such key positions – regardless of their individual abilities.

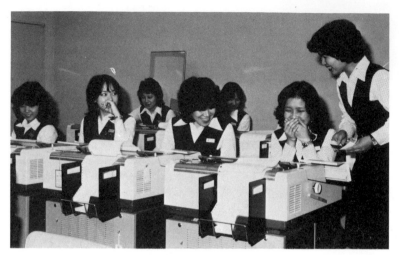

*Young women –
many of whom
will be university
graduates – seen
training for work
in the Fuji Bank.*

Employment statistics confirm that, should an intelligent and determined young woman circumvent the obstacles which stand between
her and a place in an élite university, she has little guarantee of finding
satisfactory employment when she graduates. Though women account
for more than half of the labour force (about thirty million of a total of
about fifty-three million) they are mostly concentrated in clerical and
service positions. When they do obtain senior and professional positions
it is overwhelmingly in those sectors considered to be suitable for
women, for example teaching and nursing. The typical woman worker
in fact is the 'OL', or office lady, hired to do routine office work, to pour
tea for company members several times a day, and to create a pleasant
working environment for the men who do the serious work in the office.
To add insult to injury the Labour Standards Law (enacted in 1947),
which affirms the principle of equal pay for equal work, is respected only
in the breach. The average wage of women workers is little more than
half of that received by male workers. Even in an area like transporta-
tion and communications, where women tend to do rather better, they
only receive about two-thirds of the average pay of men who are doing
the same kind of job.

The subordinate position of women in the labour market is, in part,
a consequence of the employers' belief that women look at employment,
even post-graduate employment, as a means of occupying time and
energies surplus to the central business of locating and securing a husband. The prevailing view is that women do not really need to work and
so in times of recession it is the women who are first to lose their jobs.
Harsh as this situation is for women – particularly working-class women
who are constrained to work by economic pressures, and who spend
much of their adult lives in and out of the labour market suffering the

compound ills of low pay, access mainly to the lower categories of industrial work requiring minimal skills, limited job security and the burden of doubling as wives and workers, mothers and workers – the general reluctance to take the employment of women seriously is not without justification. There is little doubt that marriage remains the overriding concern of young women between ages twenty and twenty-four and that the great majority of young women will in fact be married by the time they are twenty-five. Once past this age, indeed, a Japanese girl, if she is still unmarried, will see herself as a failure, however successful her life may seem to Western eyes. A song popularised by Frank Sinatra has crystallised the regrets and uncertainties of a generation of talented, young and single Japanese women who poured their energies into a career and who, approaching the age of thirty, have scant prospects of marriage. They are now 'too old' and an embarrassment to their employers who regard them as 'odd'. The 'My Way' philosophy rationalises the failure of these women and highlights the exaggerated emphasis which most young women still place upon marriage.

However, it is the young man rather than the young woman, and men in general more than women in general, who believe that marriage should signal the end of a woman's employment outside the home. A recent government survey reflects these views. Women of all ages accept that marriage (nineteen per cent) and more importantly childbirth (fifty-one per cent) will interrupt their working lives. But more than fifty per cent would like to return to work after bringing up their children. In contrast fifty-eight per cent of men of all ages believe that employment outside the home should be temporary and subordinate to the tasks of looking after the husband and rearing the children. Sixteen per cent of men believe that women should not work at all (eight per cent of women agree), twenty-six per cent believe that women should stop work at marriage (nineteen per cent of women agree) and sixteen per cent of men believe that women should stop work when they have children (a view shared by twelve per cent of women).

There is some evidence that women *are* returning to work after bringing up their children. If more do not return it is because the conditions which would allow women to have an occupation are not available in Japan. One of the main problems (as in this country) is the lack of adequate nursery facilities. There was already a waiting list of close on 500,000 children for the 16,300 day care centres in 1973, and the figure is now nearer 750,000. The figure would undoubtedly be greater still if many of the women who would like to work believed that it was even remotely possible that they would be able to share their domestic burdens with an institution of this kind. The problem is even more acute in the educated middle class. One of Japan's leading exponents of music therapy in the education of retarded children can only work if she teaches at home, and even then she is regarded as 'odd' by her equally educated middle class neighbours.

Slowly attitudes are changing. For the moment the majority of young women subscribe to the 'one role ideology of woman's basic inferiority and natural domesticity', whilst the 'new women' who refuse to be confined to a single role and who claim equality with men – and still more the 'radical egalitarian' women who reject traditional sex roles and traditional marriages – are at present minority groups. It has been argued, however, that even the mainstream young woman is a 'neo-traditionalist' who can be distinguished from her elder traditionalist sister by virtue of her changed attitudes to politics, education, work, and (as we shall see) marriage. The overall voting rate, which is slightly higher for women than men is, in the case of young people under the age of twenty-nine, substantially higher for women than men. This recent phenomenon (it has happened only in the last ten years) is certainly evidence of a change in attitude to political participation, and is, perhaps, evidence of a new willingness of young women to involve themselves in areas traditionally reserved for men.

Statistically, the new, politically active young woman remains insignificant. Individual cases however reveal both the poignancy and pioneering significance of women like Setsuko, whose story appears in a recent study. Setsuko grew up in a small village on the island of Shikoku. When she graduated from high school she had no particular thoughts except that some day she would get married like her girlfriends. During her last year at college, however, she became increasingly interested in the topic of her graduation essay – the safety of commercial fabrics used for clothes. She began interviewing manufacturers and consumer groups and she was shocked to find that many widely-used fabrics were flammable and dangerous. She decided that she would have to do something with the knowledge she had acquired from her research. Her family, worried about a daughter alone in Tokyo, wanted her home after graduation. In their letters they began to mention likely candidates for an arranged marriage, but Setsuko pressed to be allowed to stay and in the end her parents agreed. She accepted a job with the Housewives' Association, a leading Japanese consumer group.

And yet the magnitude of the change should not be exaggerated. An official survey of the 'Status of Women in Modern Japan' paints a very different picture, in which the young woman is apolitical, non-participatory, concerned above all with home and family. Only one per cent of young women take part in civic movements or say that they would like to join such movements in the future. Although young women are better voters than young men, only twenty-six per cent of those questioned are sufficiently interested in politics to read more than the occasional newspaper article on political and economic matters – whereas a large majority of young men claim to read such articles regularly. When questioned about topics of general interest, and favourite topics of conversation, nearly half of the young women in the survey mentioned 'love affairs and marriage' and thirty-eight per cent 'fashion'.

It is also claimed that the 'neo-traditionalist' young woman believes that the serious study of basic subjects is as necessary for girls as for boys. Certainly it is true that the home economics option is chosen by very few senior high school girls, which suggests that girls receive the same basic education as boys. However, this is not the case in higher education, where home economics is by far the most popular subject studied by one in three junior college girls, more than the combined total studying the humanities, social sciences, science, and agriculture put together. The second most popular subject, teacher training, has also traditionally been regarded as a women's subject in Japan. In fact, there is good reason to believe that young women do not see the junior college degree as an intrinsically worthwhile educational objective, or as a way of getting a better job. It has become instead 'a new kind of marriage credential that many people now see as necessary for young women of the middle class or upper-middle class who want to attract a suitable male'.

The major change in the 'neo-traditionalist' woman's attitude to work is the abandonment of the pre-war view that work is appropriate for women only when it is essential – that is, if severe family hardship was to be avoided. Today it is seen as a matter of course for a girl to take a job. Few girls now stay at home any more just preparing for marriage, and for most, says a recent study, whether for pocket money, personal enrichment, to find a husband, or to save money for a trip abroad, taking a job has come to be generally accepted as a natural and necessary stage of growing up.

Male attitudes are changing rather more slowly and remain a stumbling block – a point well-illustrated by the attempts of Japanese women students to organise a campaign to lobby Government and business to provide more jobs for women graduates. 'The Society to think about the employment of Women College Graduates' marshalled its arguments well, but when it tried to confront the male representatives of business and Government with the fact that the number of job offers for graduating women in 1976 was only one quarter of that for the corresponding period of 1975, the men in charge of the offices visited by the women's lobby refused to meet them.

Marriage, sexual morality and contraception

Both men and women have changed their views about marriage. The arranged marriage system, which has itself changed to become less formal, has declined in importance since the Second World War so that nowadays less than half of all Japanese marriages are arranged. Today the preference is for a love marriage. Even those who avail themselves of the 'fail-safe mechanism' of an arranged marriage assume the role and attitudes of 'lovers' once formal contacts have been established.

The importance attached to 'love' in contemporary Japan has not affected the young single woman's ideas of what constitutes a good spouse. Forty-two per cent of the young single women polled recently put the greatest emphasis on 'good understanding' and forty-five per cent on 'reliability'. Young women rate reliability more highly than older women (who, perhaps, are less willing to aspire after the unattainable). Most young women would prefer their husband to see them as 'a charming woman' than as a 'woman of firm character'. The views of married women are the reverse of this and much closer to the views men themselves have of a preferred wife. Among married men especially, charm is a very poor second to character but even young men consider charm less important.

There is also some evidence of a generation gap in terms of attitudes to divorce. Whereas, in the same survey, about a third of both young women and young men approved or could sympathise with divorce 'to some extent', only about twenty per cent of married men and women did so. The generation gap is equally marked over attitudes to greater sexual freedom, especially among women. This change of attitude is in line with the increased rate of divorce which, though it is still much lower than in the United Kingdom, has doubled in the last ten years. The number of separated couples has also increased sharply, so that there are now some 670,000 one-parent families in Japan. The figures for divorce underestimate the significance of these changes in attitude, which are already reflected in films and in the night life of the big cities. Bars which cater exclusively for rich, bored, middle-class housewives have sprouted in places like Tokyo. Here women receive the kind of attention from handsome, immaculately dressed, often foreign, young men which Japanese men have long received from hostesses and bar girls. Similar indications of the new fantasy life of Japanese women are the many films which package and re-package the story of the neglected housewife who finds release and fulfilment with a young and handsome college boy.

Changes in attitude are closely related to the decline of the arranged marriage and the growing popularity of love matches. In the case of the arranged marriage love was expected to develop after a couple became engaged through the good offices of a respectable go-between. The overt manifestation of love before marriage was frowned on. In such a climate there was little prospect – or, for that matter, need – for the development of practices common in the West, such as dating. When the onus of finding a partner shifted from the go-between to the individual young man or woman, dating became a social necessity. The greater frequency, informality (given the absence of the go-between), and warmth of contacts between young men and women created an environment in which new attitudes to sex and love were likely to flourish.

The sexual customs of the West were a major influence in shaping the new attitudes. In the immediate post-war period several hundred thousand GIs confirmed the existence of a very different and 'modern' sexual morality. The message they preached was taken up and reiterated by Hollywood, which had long since discovered the potency of sex and romance in drawing people to the cinemas, and the combination was to prove equally effective in Japan. With economic recovery came higher wages and increased opportunities for leisure. Things Western were hugely popular and the movie was a perfectly packaged and easily accessible slice of Western life. The film stars filled a vacuum and satisfied a need created by the uncertainties of defeat and the disappearance (or at least the 'illegitimacy') of a generation of Japanese leaders and heroes. Not surprisingly, the Japanese flocked to the cinemas where they were fed a steady diet of sex and romance – initially in the style of Vivien Leigh and Clark Gable (in *Gone with the Wind*) but subsequently 'improved' and updated in line with the evolution of sexual customs in the West through *Love Story* to *Emmanuelle*. Japanese film makers were not slow to learn from this example, so that now they too preach the message of 'sexual liberation' as insistently as Hollywood.

Changes in sexual morality are most marked in the cities – and it is precisely here that housing problems are most acute. There is much less land available for building but the demand increases annually with the overall increase in population. Only among the middle-aged and the elderly with high incomes is there a high rate of home ownership. The young with small incomes have poor – though improving – prospects of ownership. Consequently most young Japanese live at home with their parents until they get married. Much of the housing stock is old, small, cramped, and flimsily constructed. Three-generation households (married couple plus children plus parent(s), or married couple plus children plus a parent and other relatives, for example the wife's unmarried sister) are common – in some areas as many as one in three households is of this kind. Privacy is therefore minimal. Moreover, the absence of gardens – indeed of roads and pavements – in many residential areas, and the consequent proximity of neighbouring houses, makes it very difficult for a young subscriber to the new 'sexual morality' to escape the attentions of neighbours, let alone of the family. The presence in the household of respected elderly relatives further guarantees that the behaviour required of young people will be biased towards 'traditionalism' or, more loosely, 'old fashioned ideas' with which they have little sympathy. The famed indulgence of their children by Japanese parents does not, it seems, extend to sexual matters.

Not surprisingly then the young socialise outside the home. They spend an even larger proportion of their income on eating out than their parents do and tend to eat with their colleagues from the same department or section in the firm or office. Nearly all pre-marital sexual activity occurs outside the home. Public parks are favourite places. At the weekends, and particularly on Sundays, they fill with young couples strolling hand-in-hand and groups of younger children laughing, teasing, bantering, and flirting. In late evening, as the drone of city traffic is replaced by the saw-saw chorus of the cicadas, the activity intensifies and the parks become no-go areas for the middle-aged, the unaccompanied and the easily embarrassed.

The conflict between the new attitudes of the young, and the constraints of the home situation (which are perhaps even worse for the young worker in company housing or the student in a boarding house or hostel) can cause considerable distress to young adults who are involved in a serious relationship but who cannot, or do not, wish to marry. Commercial interests are more than willing to relieve that distress – temporarily, and at a price. 'Love-hotels' – elaborate confections in white, inspired (if that is the word) by Ludwig of Bavaria by way of Walt Disney have erupted, rash-like, in the major cities. Exorbitantly expensive, they are geared to the indulgence and fulfilment of the sexual fantasies of their clients – usually wealthy and middle-aged, often homosexual or lesbian, in settings which range from 'dungeon rooms' where the theme is sado-masochism and the paraphernalia whips and black leather, to 'romance rooms' in which crushed red velvet and heart-shaped beds set the tone. Though the love-hotels are beyond the means of the average young man and woman, the *'doohan kissaten'* or 'couples only' coffee shops are not. These lowly regarded, much frequented, establishments are common to all the major cities. They are known not so much for the quality of the coffee and alcoholic drinks they serve as for the dim lighting, the rows of single booths with high backs and the discretion of the staff.

The majority of young people survive this period and ninety per cent of them get married. When they do – particularly if they are city dwellers – they will live with their children and apart from their parents, thereby breaking with the tradition of the couple living with the groom's parents. They are much more likely than the older generation to see the husband and wife rather than the children as the core element in the family. But in spite of this new emphasis upon the 'horizontal' relationship between husband and wife, the 'vertical' structure which emphasises parent-child ties will remain strong. Two-thirds of all mothers living apart from their grown children see them at least once or twice a month. More than half of all elderly couples are financially dependent on their children – particularly on the eldest son.

Another important difference between the generations is that young women now want fewer children; and to achieve this contraception is indispensable. Knowledge of contraception is virtually universal in Japan, but whereas older women tended to obtain information about contraception from their husbands a majority of young wives now receive this knowledge from a health centre. Unrestricted sale of the pill is, however, illegal and the three per cent of married women who use this form of contraception do so on prescription, and at the discretion of their doctor. Authorisation of the free use of the pill has been much debated in recent years. It is a question on which the young are particularly well informed and it is likely that they favour authorisation. Although it is significant that there is a flourishing black market trade in the pill, the great majority of young couples use the condom with the rhythm method a poor second.

A substantial majority of young wives approve of abortion, not just when birth will harm the mother's life or health or in cases of pregnancy resulting from rape, but also when the birth of a child could cause serious financial difficulties, when conception is the result of a failure of contraception. A sizeable minority of young wives have actually had abortions though very few of them were unconcerned by the experience. Though the number of reported cases of abortion is declining, there is good reason to believe that there are large numbers of unreported abortions every year, and that for many young women abortion is a legitimate *contraceptive* practice free from the taboos that surround the pill. The preference for abortion over the pill perhaps reflects the uncertainties of a changing sexual morality, since the pill implies a much greater degree of premeditation and commitment than abortion.

Youth and Crime

The problem of juvenile delinquency is central to the discussion of the young and social change. Levels of juvenile crime tell us something of the willingness of the young to confine their behaviour to socially sanctioned forms. The nature of the crimes suggests the main points of friction between the young and those of society at large. Finally, by contrasting change in the juvenile crime rate with change in the adult crime rate, we get some indications about the strengthening or weakening of social discipline.

Since 1951 – remarkably, given the immediate post-war experience of other advanced industrial nations – the crime rate in Japan has continuously decreased. More specifically, the crime rate for adult offenders has decreased continuously while the rate for juvenile offenders has fluctuated. The juvenile rate decreased in line with that of adults from 1950 to 1953 – which can be partly explained by the improved

economic situation. From 1956, however, the number of both juvenile offenders and offences rose steeply, and peaked in 1964. Since then there has been a downward trend of offences and offenders among the older juveniles (eighteen to nineteen years of age), but a steady increase among the other age groups, particularly the fourteen to seventeen-year-olds.

As for the number of offenders, 163,944 young people were treated as juvenile Penal Code 'suspected' offenders in 1973. The term 'suspected' is used advisedly. The Japanese judicial system has a wide margin of discretion in its dealings with young offenders, many of whom are (as a consequence) never formally convicted by a court. Given the discretion operating throughout the system, it would be misleading to deal only with those actually convicted. In the same year (1973) the police 'investigated and gave guidance' to 38,746 children under fourteen years of age. If these young people had been fourteen – the age of criminal responsibility – they too would have been referred to the 'family court' or the public prosecutor. In addition, the police contacted and gave 'guidance and direction' to several hundred thousand children whose behaviour gave cause for concern. Parents, teachers, social workers and neighbours invited the police to intervene and deal with these 'pre-delinquent juveniles' who were smoking, drinking, indulging in 'un-wholesome pastimes', playing truant, mixing with bad company, loitering in entertainment areas, 'inhaling paint thinner', etc.

Glues and thinners have indeed replaced heroin at the heart of the drug problem in Japan. Heroin addiction, a serious problem in 1963 with an estimated 40,000 addicts, was effectively eradicated by the mid-

1970s. The use and abuse of cannabis and LSD has never involved more than a few hundred individuals in Japan. Glue-sniffing and the inhaling of thinners is quite a different matter. The official figures (which probably underestimate the scale of abuse) suggest that 50,000 young people were involved in the early 1970s and in one year nearly a hundred young people died from the consequences. The low cost of solvents, their availability and ease of use are important aspects of the attractiveness of this form of delinquency. In contrast, the young were not significantly involved in the re-emergence of amphetamines as a drug problem in the 1970s. It is interesting that there is no large drug sub-culture in Japan, nor is there any significant support for the decriminalisation of drug offences or for the legislation of the use of drugs like cannabis. Indeed the typical (and exceedingly effective) response to the resurgence of a drug problem in Japan is legislation, intensified enforcement, compulsory hospitalisation, and nationwide 'educational' campaigns. In this area, as one commentator concludes, 'Japan prefers control to toleration'.

Statistically, larceny is much more important than drug abuse. Nearly half of the juvenile 'suspects' in 1973 fell foul of the police because they had been involved in thefts. A further thirty-four per cent committed serious traffic offences, often with stolen vehicles, which resulted in death or injury. Stealing is particularly important in the lower age groups (fourteen to nineteen-year-olds) whereas older juveniles and young adults (the twenty to twenty-four age group) are more often prosecuted for assault and for causing bodily injury. The difference in the kind of offences that are committed by these two groups suggests that only a small number of young Japanese graduate to more serious crimes and become absorbed in the world of organised crime.

Explanations of the low and falling crime rate in Japan focus on the peculiarly intense pressures upon the individual to conform and to avoid bringing shame on family, friends, and associates at work. As one commentator says, 'everyone in Japan has a recognised position to fill in the scheme of things, and he is expected to live up to it. Japanese society is so constructed that if he does not live up to it, then he will be despised and bring shame on all those connected with him . . .' The sense of obligation to others – even, in the Western view, quite distant others – is underlined by the number of suicides in which the farewell note is addressed not to a spouse or lover but to an employer. The intensity of the feelings that can be aroused is startlingly illustrated by the reaction of the fathers of the Red Army Faction militants who were arrested for murder. The fathers killed themselves out of a sense of shame – shame brought on them, their families, and their colleagues, and in order to bring home to the offenders the enormity of their behaviour.

Not surprisingly, therefore, attempts to explain the fluctuating juvenile crime rate have looked for signs of change in the family, friendship network, and the workplace – the key institutional supports of the web of constraints, inhibitions, and expectations which binds the individual and prevents deviance. One study shows that the sense of involvement in, and identification with, a group based on the family or the workplace is much weaker in the juvenile delinquent than in his non-delinquent counterpart. Another, which demonstrates the relationship between the physical separation of the juvenile from the group, and his propensity to commit crime, confirms the importance of group identification and the 'feeling of belonging' in crime prevention. When these weaken, crime increases. There is, for example, a significantly higher crime rate among young people who have moved away from home to live in the cities than among those who grew up there.

Every year the young pour into the large cities – especially Tokyo – looking for jobs, places in colleges or universities, or simply in search of the excitement of city life. Very few of them have previous records of delinquency. In the city their living conditions are poor. Their strange accents mark them as different in a society which is intolerant of those who are different. At weekends and at holiday times they are socially isolated by the lack of family life. Those living apart from their parents in Tokyo are twice as likely to commit crimes as those living at home. High wages provide scant compensation for these disadvantages for, if family ties remain strong, then the lion's share of the young peoples' earnings are sent home, leaving them only limited funds on which to manage. Such a situation frequently leads to crime. The psychological and physical distancing from the family is compounded in many instances of delinquency by retreat from another group, the work place. The 'urban migrant juveniles' often have poor work records which date from the time the migrant leaves his earlier job in the town or the village to come to the city.

Juvenile delinquency remains a central problem for the Japanese. One of its major causes, the erosion of group identification, is a result of the migration of young people to the cities. There is little evidence to suggest that levels of migration will fall or that new non-deviant group identities will emerge as a substitute for the family and the work group. It can consequently be assumed therefore that juvenile crime will remain a problem for the years ahead. Since crime in general is decreasing, however, despite the fluctuations in the juvenile crime rate, today's juvenile delinquent is not necessarily tomorrow's adult offender.

Conclusion

The comprehensive change in the outward appearance of Japanese life is beyond dispute. In their dress, their leisure pursuits, and their consumption patterns, young people in Japan have come closely to resemble their

Western counterparts. But it is much less clear how far this outward transformation of life-styles has been accompanied by change in the *inner* life of young Japanese men and women. It may seem that such changes have been far from superficial; that the new consumption style has been accompanied by the spread of new values which reflect this style. In their attitudes to work, marriage, politics and sexual morality, young Japanese are moving closer to the views of young Westerners and away from those of the older Japanese – so much so indeed that it is possible to speak of the existence of a generation gap.

And yet it might be objected that this is a passing fad; that as the young people mature they will rediscover the traditional values that they rejected in their youth; that, in short, the young will grow out of their fashionable Western attitudes. Equally it might be argued that the distance which still separates young Japanese from young Westerners is more striking than the degree of convergence; that in his attachment to work the young Japanese man, and in her expectations of education and work the young Japanese woman, remain more in tune with the values of the older generation in Japan than with their young counterparts in the West. Though there is certainly some truth in both of these objections, there is some evidence that the new values are not abandoned as the young mature – young student radicals for example remain committed to their fundamental political beliefs well into adulthood.

Even more important than the tenacity with which the young hold on to their new values are the changes in the social supports of traditional values. The weakening of the sense of identity with a group based on the family or the workplace for example fosters the growth of criminal behaviour. It is at least possible therefore that the movement away from the extended family to the nuclear family, the emergence of new values in the workplace and in politics, and the changed economic circumstances of a post oil-crisis world will further erode the social foundations of older values. The only certainty is that Japan and the Japanese will continue to change and that the young will be at the very centre of the process. The likelihood is, surely, that some (though certainly not all) of the new values will take root, either because of their inherent desirability or because of their compatibility with older values.

3
The continuity of Japanese culture
Geoffrey Bownas

Introduction

Their homogeneity, and their awareness of it, is one of the most striking features of the Japanese. There is one people, one language; there is even one culture, which all claim to appreciate. Japan's homogeneity is largely the consequence of her geographical isolation. Although the Japan Sea is only 125 miles across at its narrowest point, it has always proved inhospitable enough to both invader and immigrant to preserve Japan's individuality intact from about the fourth century BC until General MacArthur landed in 1945.

This homogeneity, too, helps to explain the pride that the Japanese take in their unique culture – a pride so intense that at times it may easily slide into arrogance. This arrogance is evident in the thinking of a number of Japanese who claim that the spirit of their culture is too refined for the outsider to understand – particularly the outsider who does not share Japan's oriental heritage. As one philosopher, writing in the 1930s, said, 'the fondness of the Japanese for astringency, the elegant simplicity of all his tastes in food, clothes and dwelling conditions, his attitude to the moderation and the charm in everyday behaviour – these are all too refined and delicate for the European to appreciate'.

Another consequence of Japan's unique homogeneity is the easy and fluent transmission of a common mood to other minds. A shared and intuitive 'meeting of feeling' between sympathetic and sensitive minds allows a gathering of three or four *haiku* poets to pool their sensitivity and to contribute link verses to a common poem without it descending to the level of a mere 'scrabble'. (In fact, *haikai*, one of the highest literary forms of the seventeenth and eighteenth centuries, was usually such a composite creation.) This easy transfer of mood also makes a Japanese concert audience the most intense in the world; and it creates a highly charged emotional event out of a gathering such as the opening ceremony of the Tokyo Olympic Games in 1964.

The homogeneous Japanese that we know today are, however, the descendants of an earlier racial mixture. It seems certain that two quite distinct migratory waves peopled the Japanese islands. One came eastwards across the top of Asia, leaving its mark on the structure of the language and on religious practice. The other wave flowed north or northeastwards from southern China and the islands of southeast Asia. Many of the elements of traditional culture that remain today were brought by this stream from the south. Rice-growing, as the basis of agriculture, was one of these elements. And in architecture, even today, for example, a house built in the traditional style (and many are, by those who wish to conserve the indigenous as a kind of status symbol) is planned with an eye to tolerating the humidity and claggy heat of Japan's summer rather than to resisting the piercing cold of her winter. The house may be lifted a foot or two above ground level on stilts (to allow the free passage of air below, as well as to take earthquake strain), and all its internal partitions either slide open or can be removed completely, in order to catch every slight stir of air on a stifling midsummer evening; but against the winter cold traditional domestic architecture has produced no effective barrier. This traditional style is also visible in early public buildings that are still extant; the Shōsōin (the repository of Imperial treasures) of the eighth century was built on stilts in the *azekura* (loghouse) style–allowing the free passage of air underneath to prevent damage from humidity, and protecting the treasures from the damp air of summer by tight fitting log construction. The continuity of Japanese culture and the conscious imitation of the past is well illustrated by the façade of the National Theatre, built in 1966 in a modern interpretation of the 'loghouse' style, and the home of *kabuki* and other traditional performing arts. Again, most traditional forms of Japanese cooking suit the heat of summer rather than the cold of winter – cold rice in a variety of forms, and astringent pickles, cold raw fish. Traditional clothing, too, matches the summer. For winter additional layers are added, or padded and quilted linings are inserted; there is no basic change of style.

Japan's culture is also terminal. Japan lies at the end of the culture route which begins sometimes in India, or more often in China, and which reaches Japan either directly from China or via Korea or the northern limits of Asia. The barrier of the Japan Sea has meant that Japan has been able to incorporate from the rest of Asian culture what and when she chose. She could reject out of hand anything that seemed not to match her temperament and she could adapt what she borrowed – and she early became adept at giving these loans a peculiarly Japanese character. Again, she could sever her links completely with the source of

The priests of the great Yasukuni Shrine in Tokyo assemble for the spring rite of Shintō.

her cultural loans (as she did, on several occasion, with China and later with the West) and withdraw into herself.

Japanese culture is, finally, cumulative. The Japanese tradition is almost always growing and moving. A whole civilisation was adopted from China, and a wide variety of new ideas has come from the West in the past century, but these borrowings are always ingested, moulded to the tradition and added to the corpus. The cumulative character of Japan's culture enables it to absorb and blunt the force of change. This is the source both of the continuity of the canon and of the authority inherent in the basic elements of the tradition. Japan's cultural history has no catastrophic endings, no dramatic new beginnings. There is never a critical moment where radical change or revolution becomes inevitable. Such drastic change is not part of the Japanese process and, rather than eliminate, the Japanese would prefer to preserve two similar institutions in parallel or to put them together in synthesis. Two major religions, Buddhism and Shintō, have managed to co-exist peacefully in Japan for nearly fifteen hundred years. There have never been the major confrontations, let alone the religious wars, that have punctuated the history of the Christian world. Rather, Buddhism and Shintō (the indigenous religion) were brought together to such an extent that, at

some periods, the Buddhist and Shintō pantheon were interpreted as a dual manifestation of the same basic faith.

The cyclical development of Japanese culture

The cumulative character of Japanese culture is well illustrated by the way in which it has developed in a series of cycles. First, there is a period when the country is opened to external influences (from China or the West) and incorporates from outside on a broad scale, underrating or neglecting (though never jettisoning) native values. Then the Japanese stand back a little and examine these alien elements more closely,

*The great bronze
statue of Buddha
at Tōdaiji Temple
in Nara. The
statue, which was
cast in AD 749,
is 53 feet tall ;
the thumb alone
is more than
five feet high.*

choosing those they feel to be the most appropriate. In the course of this process of selection, the Japanese come to reassess their own values and these are used to give their borrowings a distinctively Japanese stamp. This process of synthesis then prompts the flowering of a new creation, uniquely Japanese and governed by the traditional canons and rules of taste. There follows a period in which the innovative urge is blunted and the Japanese settle into a mould of dull conformity, finally withdrawing into themselves and shutting out the world. Then, as Japan emerges from her cocoon and begins to borrow from the world again, another round of the cycle begins.

This cycle recurs repeatedly in Japan's cultural history. The first began with the close and continuous contacts with China which took place between the sixth and ninth centuries AD. During these years, Japan took an entire civilisation from China – a religion (Buddhism), a script (there was no indigenous writing system), a language (Chinese came to stand alongside Japanese as the scholar's and official's language), and a complete system of administration and urban planning. An intricate system of land tenure was established on the Chinese pattern and both Nara and Kyōto (Japan's capital cities between the eighth and twelfth centuries), with their chequer-board streets and broad boulevards, were replicas of the Chinese Imperial capital at Ch'ang-an. The jaunty, self-assured spirit of the age is perhaps best typified by the persistence that drove the Japanese, through a long succession of failures, to final success in casting a bronze statue of Buddha, fifty-three feet tall, in AD 749. Not for the last time, contact with the outside world and adoption of its skills led the Japanese to develop their own brand of techniques and the confidence to exploit them.

The loans of the *Nara period (710–794)* were assimilated and refined in the *Heian age (794–1185)*. Contacts with China became less frequent and the Heian (Kyōto) court nobles, urbane and confident, living at peace (the meaning of the word *heian*) in the world's largest capital, created a tradition so sure and so exquisite that its essential outline has survived virtually intact for a thousand years. Essentially, this tradition combined an elegant and decorous refinement, which inevitably finds the mean, with an element of graceful humour which always retains its poise and never descends to the trite.

The spirit of this culture is perhaps best expressed in the short, thirty-one syllable poem of the period. In such a short poem, not a syllable could be wasted, and a mood was created by the use of pivot-words (like a hinge – opening in two directions, with a different sense for each) which, though essentially a pun, conveyed an elegant form of wit. In the same way, there were techniques of allusion and hint, or assonantal or alliterative repetition which moved the sensibility of the age. Something of this mood comes across even in translation:

Narihira then set out for the hunt. Yet, as he walked over the moors, his thoughts were inattentive and he could think only of his longing to be with her again that night, when all would be asleep. However, the Provincial Governor of Ise invited him to a banquet which lasted through the night and Narihira was unable to meet her. He shed secret, sorrowing tears, but they were of no avail.

Just as dawn came, she sent him the leave-taking cup. A poem was written inside it:

> Shallow our union –
> Shallow as the inlet
> You walk unwet.

The final couplet was missing. Narihira wrote it on the wine cup, using the tip of a charred pine torch.

> Over Meeting Hill Barrier
> Again I shall climb to you

It was the touching, pathetic aspects of their world that most appealed to the courtier poets of the Heian period. Their response was almost always tinged with a sense of passive regret and gentle melancholy. This is the meaning of the Japanese word *aware*, the sad quality of fleeting beauty and the melancholy that it evokes. Taste or 'mood' words such as *aware*

Left
The garden of the Imperial Villa at Katsura in Kyōto. The tree has been carefully pruned to create a sense of natural harmony.

Above
The Moss Garden at Saihōji Temple, also in Kyōto. The moss flows over the natural swell of the ground and the trees bring a powerful contrast to the landscape.

recur over and over again in the story of the development of the Japanese aesthetic, and often help to pinpoint the mood of a historical or cultural period, and that of the social class that created and guided the taste of the day. *Aware* is still there today in many of the sights and sounds of Japan – perhaps in the mood of a temple landscape garden, in the fleeting beauty of falling blossom, or in the lush damp green of a moss carpet after a sharp summer evening shower; or, again, in the poignant tone of the *koto* (a horizontal harp) or the sad *shakuhachi* (flute), both instruments representative of the Heian period.

It was also during the Heian period that there developed an indigenous prose style, confident and self-assured. Typically, literature was episodic. Belles lettres, occasional jottings, and literary or poetic diaries were evolved in this period, and even the most famous novel of the age, *The Tale of Genji*, divides into a collection of separate chapters or episodes, with little in the form of a link other than the main character, Prince Genji. This episodic character of Japanese writing was to last – and is still prominent today. The fact that many contemporary novels first appear as serials in the newspapers or in weekly or monthly journals also forces an episodic format on writers.

Japan's detachment from the outside world deepened during the *Kamakura period (1192–1333)*. There is a world of difference between the urbane polish and carefree unconcern of the spirit of the culture of the Heian period and the intensity and gloom of these years – Japan's Middle Ages. This reflected the stark contrast between the moods of the groups which dictated contemporary tastes. Kamo no Chōmei (d. 1216), a one-time court poet who relinquished the fine things in life in favour of the Buddhist priesthood, had lived through the agonies of the civil wars that closed the Heian period and led to the rise of a quasi-military government based on the newly-risen *samurai* (knightly) class. His *Hōjōki* (*A Record of My Hut*) is a collection of reminiscences which starts with a progression of thoughts that captures the spirit of the times. There is no longer the carefree gaiety of the Heian courtier, when there was nothing wrong with his world; now, there is the gloom that reflects the despair of the Middle Ages.

> The river flows on and on, yet its water is never the same. The froth that rides on the backwaters vanishes and is born again, but does not live for long. So also, the world over, are men and the houses they build. Among the stately buildings of the capital, ranging roof on roof, vying tile with tile, the houses of the high or humble may seem to outlive generation after generation, never to fall in ruins. Yet few are the houses that have stood long. Either they burnt down a year ago and were rebuilt only this year, or vast mansions have toppled to become meagre huts . . .

The mood of this passage is best described by the Japanese taste word *sabi*, which, like *aware* and other 'mood' words, is still in regular currency. *Sabi* contains the sense of both rust (or patina, as on old bronze) and of loneliness; perhaps, to adopt an artifice typical of the Japanese, 'patinated loneliness'.

After the fall of the feudal military house based on Kamakura (in the east, near the modern Tokyo), the administrative centre returned to Kyōto (Muromachi, an area of Kyōto, gave its name to the age) and Japan once again began to look outward. It was during the *Muromachi period (1333–1573)* that nearly all of the elements of the tradition that survive today and are labelled as most typically Japanese came into being. Buddhism, and particularly the Zen sect, the sect of the *samurai*, helped shape the arts. It also inspired new creative forms such as the tea ceremony; this art, in its turn, profoundly influenced the crafts and skills of others such as the potter, painter, or architect.

Most Buddhist sects preach salvation through reliance on, and faith in, an external agent beyond the self. By contrast, the Zen sect made man

The Imperial Palace in Kyōto. The use of space is a crucial element in the relationship of the buildings with their surrounding landscape.

seek the Buddha nature within himself. He should look inside, understand himself and attain enlightenment by meditation (*zazen* in Japanese). Introspection is the prelude to a sudden flash of enlightenment (*satori*), which is neither capable of verbal expression nor to be achieved by the logical progression of intellectual concepts. So a Zen master would set problems (*kōan*) for his novices of the kind that were not amenable to solution by the intellect and that would jolt him out of reliance on reason. So the Zen route to truth was by way of an intuitive jump, spurred by introspection, beyond and denying all logic. Zen Buddhism, with its self-examination and its preference for intuitive empathy over intellectual cognition, lies at the heart of Japanese culture.

The Tea Ceremony

Introduced in the fifteenth century, the tea ceremony appealed as a refined pleasure, away from life's bustle, to powerful warrior lords or increasingly wealthy merchants. The art of tea-drinking was perfected in the sixteenth century by Sen no Rikyū (a citizen of Sakai, the most developed commercial centre at the time). The tea-house itself, calling for new skills in the architect, was an expression of two of the tastes and moods prized at the time – *wabi* (quiet taste) and *shibumi* (severe sobriety). The plain, thatched simplicity of the tea-house contrasted starkly with the florid splendour of the warlord's castle. It had dark sliding doors, covered with panes of soft, white translucent Japanese paper; the wood of pillars was left in its natural state, bark and all. The ceiling was of latticed bamboo or reed and a high value was put on the balance created by the bare texture of the walls.

This same severe beauty soon came to be sought in the tea bowls, jars and vases, bamboo whisks and ladles and other utensils that went with the tea ceremony. There was also the sombre calm created around the tea-house by the landscape gardener, and inside it by the artist or calligrapher who painted the scroll which, hung in the alcove, was the only form of decoration on the tea-house walls. Finally, the art of flower arrangement was linked to the tradition of the tea ceremony. Ikenobō Senkei, who introduced flower arrangement into the tea house, sought to intensify the 'mood' of the tea ceremony by expressing in his arrangements a purity and simplicity which would help the participant to penetrate the depths of nature.

The heroine of 'Dōjōji', a famous Nō play, at the dedication ceremony of a new temple bell under which she will later be transformed into a serpent.

Nō

Perfected by Seami in the fifteenth century, and deeply influenced by the tenets and aesthetics of the Zen sect, *Nō* drama was the typical literary product of the age. It is perhaps the supreme example of the ascetic economy and controlled restraint that are so often associated with the Japanese tradition. *Nō* is a blend of speech, music and dance; perfection in performance attained a 'suggested beauty, elusive and tinged with wistfulness'. A *Nō* performance achieves a perfect balance between forces. The beat of the percussion instruments links intricately with chanted word and dance posture and a flute *obbligato* sets the mood for each of the three movements of a play, introduction, development and climax – something like sonata form in western music. *Nō* plays often have two scenes, the ghostly spirit world and the world of the present; the mood of the musical accompaniment and the voicing of the chorus can be hardened to express the chasm separating the two and the anguish of the journey between them, while in the closing music a mellow tone assists catharsis and the resolution of madness.

The supreme attainment of a *Nō* performance is *yūgen* – a dark, suggested beauty, obscure and elusive, only half-revealed and tinged with wistfulness. Here, in one art form and in the taste word that best expresses it, are all the qualities which constitute the uniqueness of Japanese culture. But the Japanese have not found a satisfactory definition; it is near to symbolism, but there is a tendency to take us to the threshold of *yūgen* with statements of *yūgen*-ful thoughts or moments and leave us standing there unanswered. *Yūgen* has long defied the would-be definer. This was said of it in 1430:

> *Yūgen* may be comprehended by the mind, but it cannot be expressed in words. Its quality may be suggested by the sight of a thin cloud veiling the moon or by autumn mist swathing the scarlet leaves on a mountainside. If one is asked where in these sights lies the *yūgen*, one cannot say . . .

For Seami (1363–1443) it seems that it was sometimes the moments of 'non-action' that most nearly achieved the perfection of *yūgen* in a *Nō* performance. When it is a question of intuition, beyond all logic, the eternity beyond movement and gesture is not to be suggested or conveyed by an actor's action, but rather by the spiritual strength which is revealed in his non-action.

In the final century of the Muromachi period, military leaders established in local strongholds struggled for supremacy and civil war became endemic. Finally, in 1603, Tokugawa Ieyasu emerged victorious. For the greater part of the *Edo period (1603–1867)*, which followed, Japan was completely and deliberately shut off from external influences. It was a period, at the start, of great creativity and later of almost complete stultification. Here was Japan as an 'octopus-pot' society, as it has been described by Maruyama Masao, one of Japan's leading political theorists. Once in your octopus pot (like our Western lobster pot) you cannot find an escape route; all values are introversive and subjective, and there is no path to other groups and the resultant cross-fertilisation and criticism. (The converse, according to Maruyama, is the rake-type society of the West; each unit is a prong and these interlink and lead back to the handle which acts both as line of communication and as arbiter of common standards.) During the Edo period the whole nation was, in a sense, cooped up in a single octopus pot, unable and unwilling to communicate with those outside.

It was the 'townsman' who created an exciting and different new culture in the first decades of the Edo period. There were new forms of fiction, the puppet theatre (*bunraku*), *kabuki* theatre and *haiku* poetry – all of them, in origin, a protest, an escape from earlier tradition and a reflection of the perky ways and spirited mood of the 'townsmen' themselves. The 'townsman' was the merchant or the man who provided services and skills in the new urban centres such as Osaka and Edo (the old name for Tokyo). Untaxed and increasingly affluent, the merchant created an outlet for his wealth in his own class culture. His art forms reflected his way of life – *ukiyo*, the 'life of the floating world'. *Ukiyoe* (pictures of the floating world) painters and printers found their themes in contemporary life and manners, in the demi-monde of the *geisha*, in *sumo* wrestling and in the *kabuki* theatre.

Two scenes from the famous Kabuki *play – 'Nozakimura'.*

Above – Omitsu with her father and the lover who will desert her for the beautiful girl from the city – below.

Kabuki

Kabuki drama, developing alongside and deriving some of its techniques from the puppet theatre, dealt primarily with two types of theme, the historical or legendary drama and the play about contemporary life. The plots of these contemporary dramas were sometimes based on actual events, and often dealt with 'type' themes – the favourite being the conflict between heart and duty. Such themes were often significant in the life of the 'townsman', and plays based on actual events were both popular and dramatically touching. *The Love Suicides at Sonezaki*, for instance, the work of the great 'townsman' dramatist Chikamatsu in the early eighteenth century, was built round the double suicide of a courtesan and the employee of a soya sauce merchant, and was staged less than a month after the event. It even quotes snatches of contemporary popular songs.

Male actors played female parts (and have developed a remarkably skilful tradition). There was a chanter who spoke for the main actors and narrated the passage of events at high points in the drama; his voice fluctuates in tempo and tone according to the moment in the drama, and chimes in with the notes of the *samisen* (the three-stringed instrument, like a guitar and plucked with a plectrum, which had come from the Ryūkyū Islands just before the beginning of the Edo period). There are often many minor parts and there is much movement and clatter from groups of warriors or porters. By the second half of the eighteenth century, there had also been remarkable developments in the technique of staging *kabuki* – there were elaborate sets, and advanced stage machinery included a revolve and stage lifts. The lavish colour and extravagant

staging represent a major contrast with the economy and restraint of *Nō* drama. Costume was elaborate, colours often novel and contrived specially for a new play. One leading actor of the early nineteenth century, Rokō, wore a new shade of brown in a play written specially for him and, within a week, every merchant's lady who regarded herself as in tune with fashion was wearing something in Rokō brown.

Towards the end of *Love Suicides at Sonezaki* there occurs a *michiyuki* passage (lovers' journey) in poetic form of alternating five and seven syllable lines which is regarded as one of the most poetic passages in the whole of puppet and *kabuki* drama. After Tokubei and Ohatsu (the courtesan) have decided to kill themselves, the *michiyuki* scene describes their journey to the place they have chosen for their suicide. At this high point in the drama, the chanter has a major role:

> *Chanter:* To this world, farewell.
> To the night, too, farewell.
> He who goes to his death
> Is as frost on the path
> To the burial ground,
> With every step melting away.
> This dream of a dream is sad.
> Ah! count the chimes –
> Seven mark the dawn
> And six have tolled;
> The one that remains –
> Last fading echo in this life,
> The bell echoing
> Joy to come beyond our death.
> Not to the bell alone,
> To grass, to trees,
> To sky, too, farewell.
> For the last time, they look up –
> Clouds, too, are heedless;
> On the water surface
> Plough star reflected bright,
> Wife and Husband stars
> In the River of heaven.
>
> *Chanter:* And now they hear the song.[1]
> 'Why will you not
> Take me as your wife?
> You may think of me as
> One you can do without.'
> We may love, we may grieve,

But fortune and the world
Are not as we would have them.
Every day it is so; until today
Never was there a day, a night,
When my heart rested,
Tortured by a love I should not feel.
'Why, oh why, is it so?
Not for an instant can I forget.
Should you wish to reject me
And go your way, it shall not be so.
Lay your hand on me, kill me,
Then leave – only thus
Shall I leave you free.'[1]
Thus she sobbed through her tears.

Tokubei: How soon our end. Before the dawn,
To die in Tenjin Grove.

Ohatsu: Sad that this year
Is for us both ill-starred –
Twenty-five for you, for me nineteen,[2]
A token of our close-linked fates,
That loves and stars should be as one.
Vows to spirits and the Buddha,
Said for this life, now
I say for a life to come –
That in that world
We share a lotus.

Chanter: Nine twelves the beads[3]
In her rosary, rubbed and told.
By their side, a greater score
Of jewel tear-drops.
Nine twelves the worldly lusts,
Passions, sorrows never spent,
But this world's journey over.
From their hearts, a black shade
In the sky. The wind is dead.
They come to Sonezaki Grove.
There? Here? They clear the grass,
Damp with dew already fallen,
Dew – to die as soon as they.

1 The words of a popular contemporary ballad.
2 Twenty-five and forty-two are still regarded as dangerous years for men, with nineteen
  and thirty-three similarly for women.
3 There are 108 beads in a Buddhist rosary, to number the sufferings born of the passions.

Haiku

Haiku, the poetry of 'townsman' culture, is a three-line form in seventeen syllables. Its development epitomizes both the continuity and the cumulative nature of the Japanese tradition. The head poem in a linked series (*haikai*), it began as a light and humorous form, an escape from the tedious confines that had come to inhibit the traditional thirty-one syllable form. But soon, by the end of the seventeenth century, in the hands of the master Bashō, it was refined and assimilated with the Japanese canon. Although *haiku* stayed close to everyday life in Bashō's hands (frog and flea taking the place of falling blossom and misted moon, for instance), it so treated the particular in its scant seventeen syllables as to allow an intuitive insight into the world of the universal. Here was a close link with Zen – the compression of the vastness of nature into a confined space: here, too, was the intuitive spark, beyond and denying logic.

In some of the most telling *haiku*, the three lines paint three situations – the permanent, a momentary impingement, and the point of intersection of the two. Bashō's most famous *haiku* is of this pattern.

Furu ike ya	Old pond
Kawazu tobikomu	Frog plunging
Mizu no oto	Water-sound

U and *o* are the more dreamy, indistinct vowels of the Japanese language; *k* is the most stark of the consonants, and *a* the vowel that is used to express clarity and lucidity. (Such moods and tones are communicated to all men of sense by that 'meeting of feeling' described earlier.) So the

Kabuki *is an all-male preserve. One of the actors playing a woman – an* Onnagata *– is seen here making up for his part.*

Japanese intuition is sparked by a variety of signals – the three-plane element and the start of the poem in the still stagnation of the pond, the starkness of the frog splash and the return (in the assonance on *o* in *no oto*) to stillness after the final ripple. Here, again, is *sabi*, the taste word most appropriate to *haiku*.

Language also helps the *haiku* poet make his intuitive leap from particular to universal. Verbs need not be committed to time, tense, person, or number. In other words, *haiku* is free of the constraints of normal relationships and the poet can escape to his seventeen-syllable limbo in his world of the universal, freed from the commitments of everyday intercourse of life on the plane of the particular. This further refinement in the handing on of a tradition is fundamentally Japanese – and a far cry from the motives of the creators of 'townsman's culture'.

Haiku shows how it is allusion, intuition, and emotion that appeal to the Japanese sensibility; their place in the Western tradition is taken by logic and order. Some writers make great play of the relationship between Japan's culture, the wildness of her monsoon climate and the savagery of her countryside.

Landscape gardening

It is in this wildness in nature – the tangle of lush summer growth for instance – that prevents the natural and the orderly from going hand in hand. So, in creating beauty within their natural world, the Japanese extend the tendencies of nature and make their appeal to the senses and the emotions. To impose regularity and precision on nature – even if this attracted the Japanese spirit – would call for inconceivable expenditure of time and labour. As a consequence, the arts of the Japanese and of the Western landscape gardener differ radically. The Western tradition is rooted in logic and order and strives for man-made geometrical precision. Trees are shaped uniformly, there is a regular precision in the pattern of flower beds, lines are immaculately straight, curves perfectly rounded. Man's skill should dominate the natural and impose on it an order even more perfect than is already inherent in it.

But the art of the Japanese natural landscaper (such as Muso Sōseki for instance, who laid out the gardens of Saihōji, the Moss Temple in Kyōto) aims not to dominate but to follow and to extend the natural. A typical Japanese garden may grow from a base of moss. But the moss surface does not form a simple plane, as would a tidily clipped Western lawn; instead, it wells and undulates, following the uneven contours of the ground below. It offers a whole range of different greens, blending and contrasting with each other, in place of the monotone of the grass of a Western garden. From this moss base grows a single tree or shrub – not the serried rows or studied rings of the West. The tree may be fashioned

Scenes in the garden of Saihōji Temple in Kyōto.

to provide a blending of forces within the garden, but it retains its own natural entity because its shape is extended from the natural; it is not clipped or distorted to meet the precepts of symmetry or geometrical unity. Stones, too, growing from the moss it seems, assist the blending and balancing of forces within the whole. The intervals between them and their positioning suggest all of nature itself. This new style of gardening, like the monochrome landscape painting of the age and like *haiku*, compressed the vastness of nature into a confined space.

Painting and calligraphy

A similar aesthetic governs the emotions that guide the art of the painter or calligrapher (both use the same brush). There is no affinity with the logic and order of Rome and the Renaissance. Rather, there is a balance based on a subjective, personal (yet universally felt) and illogical sense of what looks right; there is no room here for rational techniques such as perspective or symmetry. A scroll painting, for instance, on a mellowed silk ground. Just fifteen strokes of the brush. Seven achieve a branch of bamboo, two wispy twigs and seven leaves; the other eight brush marks outline a small bird perched on the bamboo, a bold, tufted crest, a long pointed beak, accentuated legs, a dull surface for the breast and richly blackened rump and tail. The balance between the opaque, undecorated surface and the light and shade of the brushwork is achieved intuitively, not by any order or rule. Indeed, the asymmetry would not be a defect in Japanese eyes; nor would an accidental blurring of thick and thin ink tones and one stroke by a brush almost dry. (In fact, it requires a Westerner to note these points – and, in his eyes, defects.)

> Western food –
> Every damn' plate
> Faultless, round.*

Intuition, melancholy and the meeting of feeling

Asymmetry lures the Japanese. The regularity of western symmetry is boring, even annoying. In Japan, even the man who produces everyday articles – pots and plates – shuns the West's logical uniformity. In the West, a teacup or plate must fit the pattern, or be ranked as a 'second', a 'special purchase' bought in for the January sales. To the Japanese, an accident in firing that produces an irregularity in shape or a dribble in the gloss affords the appeal of the uniquely irregular and 'the natural'. Regularity of pattern and shape is cold, calculatedly mechanical; it has no attraction for Japanese intuition.

---

* A twentieth century *senryū*, a seventeen syllable form which became popular in the latter half of the Edo period, biting and humorous. The form persists today.

This intuition inclines to the simple, the natural. Indeed, in Shintō, purity (the ritual purity of the clean body, not the pure heart) is paramount, and it is the natural that approaches nearest to the pure. Jiun, an eighteenth century Buddhist priest, defined Shintō in terms of its lack of artifice, its Japaneseness – 'The way of our country is purely natural. This pure naturalness, this spontaneity, we call Shintō'.

The Japanese have always lived very close to the natural. Man merges with nature. The verandah of a Zen sect hermitage, at Shisendō in the northeastern suburbs of Kyōto, for instance, leads imperceptibly, with no break between them, to the garden. Nor is there a barrier between garden and natural hillside beyond. Shisendō's roof is thatch, light-absorbing, and sweeps low to give shade from the sun and shadow across the rake-patterned swirl of the white sand which acts as conductor between the dull, darkened wood of the verandah and the garden. The garden has a tall camellia and a variety of greens, 'humid', cooling in the summer swelter. At the edge of the garden, a clear stream glides down a bank of moss and pours into a section of bamboo tube; as the tube fills, it swings on a fulcrum and the water-weighted end tips on to a stone below with a dull 'plop'. This is the only man-made sound – but the air is loud with the screech of cicadas. As you sit on the verandah, you sense immediately how close you are to nature.

Here, too, is that gentle melancholy that is at the heart of traditional Japanese culture. Such *aware* often became the overwhelming ideal that crowded out other aesthetic aims. In poetry, for example, one looks and longs in vain for the indignation, the bite, the intellectual searching, the ecstasy in beauty or the moral zeal that have fired poets in other cultures.

In traditional music, too, there is this same monotone – or even unison, literally – of melancholy. (There is no harmonic tradition in Japan; of all Japanese musical instruments only the *shō*, a pipe organ blown by the mouth, is scored for harmony; voice and instrument or instruments in ensemble are invariably scored on the same notes.) After something like a month in Japan, I find myself craving the sort of musical experience that Japan cannot provide – at least from its native inspiration – the sheer ecstasy, almost swamping, of a B Minor Mass in York Minster, or the earthiness of Beatles LP. A fair proportion of Japanese pop music, even, is based on this same mood of melancholy.

Yet this melancholy is at the heart of a shared Japanese experience. Only those who lack all taste can fail to feel it or ignore its pull. This brings us back to that unique 'meeting of feeling' shared by the Japanese which I mentioned earlier. As we have seen, certain aspects of linguistic usage, commonly appreciated, assist such 'meeting'. And there are others. The Japanese look inside themselves (they are great narcissists), analyse their mood as they react to a natural scene and respond with delicately and closely phrased feelings. Their language makes this easier. It is finely tuned to convey the 'feel' of things and to assist the most minute examination of mood. In Japanese, for example, the function of flexion (verbal and adjectival) is not to determine the time of an action or attribute (I *do*, *did*, or *shall* go), but to hint at the degree of doubt or certainty in an act or state of mind or emotional response (I *might*, or *may perhaps not*, feel saddened or hurt). This sensitivity to mood and easy transference of sensation is universal, part of the national empathy; again, the 'meeting of feeling'.

The last hundred years

The most recent cycle in the development of Japanese culture began in the 1860s and was this time telescoped into less than a century. With the establishment of a new form of government centred on the Emperor, in 1868, Japan was reopened to external contact and influence. Immediately, there was energetic and indiscriminate aping of the West in many of the arts. By the 1880s, however, there had been time to reflect and the process of assimilating and Japanising these loans began. Some of the loans fitted the Japanese tradition and have been long-lasting. The 'I Novel', for instance, could be interpreted as being based on French Naturalism, which deeply influenced Japanese literature in the early years of the twentieth century. But it also had firm roots in the strengths of the Japanese language and in traditional literary forms (the short poem or the poetic diary, for instance), in which the writer looked into himself and wrote of his feelings as he responded to a situation, an event or another person. There were many syntheses in these years, in the novel, poetry, and music, for instance.

Japan remained receptive to outside influences until the end of the 1920s. However, as the country became politically isolated during the 1930s, so also there was a cultural withdrawal from the West. During the Pacific War, it was even regarded as an 'un-Japanese activity' to use foreign words – and a great number of these had crept into the language since the late nineteenth century. It was permissible to *play* baseball – the enemy's game – but new Japanese words replaced technical terms such as 'strike' and 'ball'. There is a bitter and sardonic savagery in the treatment of this ban on outside words in a left-wing poem of the 1930s:

> Who is he –
> The bastard who keeps yarping on that 'bar' is English?
> Isn't there a worthy Japanese word for it?
> *Sake*-spot
> And the beer they're drinking?
> That is barley-brew.
> Or, better, wheat-wine to our Fascist friends.

As Japan had been isolated from the outside world since the early 1930s, the effects of her reopening to external influences and contacts in 1945 were very dramatic. Recognising at once how much of international cultural developments they had missed, the Japanese not only became acutely susceptible to all manner of external influences but avidly adopted western values – the values of the victor, for nothing succeeds like success in Japan. Some warned about the heady, feverish fervour for everything alien to the tradition of East Asia, and some, from the depths of the abject nihilism that marked the reaction to defeat, commented sourly on the effects of the borrowings from the West:

> *Song of the tart*
> The very day the war ended
> At the burnt-out, smoke-grimed street corners,
> Unannounced, there you were –
> I saw you, loafing and loitering
>
> Where did you come from?
> Or rather, through the long war, where
> Did you hide yourselves?
> And how could you change so swiftly?
>
> You, distorted, only half there, gross,
> An almost brutal joke: but so sudden to me
> That it is beyond any joke.
> All I wish is to be shocked,
> Then to shock you.
>
> To silence all – half-hearted humanism
> And literature, fussy, fidgety politics,
> Smart theories – silence every one of them.
>
> Knees pressed into shoes, tubs, mortars –
> That is the feel you give me,
> You, your gory lips
> Puffing Chesterfields,
> Cudding chewing gum
>
> Gaping yawn from a tart,
> Red O,
> And in that O, black gloom,
> Flesh-red gloom.
>
> She yawns, fit
> To swallow a man whole.
> Never in Japan a crater
> As gaping as this yawn.

Wordy, tedious debates,
War guilt, liberalism,
All these, flung into the abyss
Of that tart's yawn,
Leave only a ripple.

But the process of indiscriminate borrowing continued well into the 1950s, beyond the San Francisco Peace Treaty and Japan's official return to peaceful relations with America and the West; it lasted, too, beyond the Korean War and the start of Japan's economic recovery. It was not until 1956, as the Japanese often say themselves, that they 'calmed down' and regained that degree of composure necessary for them to be able to stand back dispassionately and reassess the worth of the indigenous values hurriedly thrown overboard in 1945. This opportunity to halt and take stock had not occurred earlier simply because there was not the leisure to spare for emotional, intellectual or aesthetic frills after they had surmounted the severe practical problems of staying alive. When you could die of malnutrition, as did one Supreme Court judge, by living scrupulously on the rations, there was little room for anything beyond the here and now.

The synthesis of the 1960s

Japan's new composure in the late 1950s led into the synthesis of the 1960s during which the new influences borrowed from outside were absorbed, digested, and blended with the tradition. Here is yet another instance of the cumulative nature of Japan's cultural development; no hasty or wholesale jettisoning which could not be revoked, no sudden departure which did not have some roots in the tradition.

One product of the synthesis was a steadily increasing contribution by Japan to the development of the arts on the international scene. In music, for instance, there was the fruitful and imaginative blend of skill in Japan's traditional instruments or ensembles with Western techniques of composition which inspired men like Yuize Shin'ichi. Yuize, master of the *koto* and *samisen*, leader of a school deeply rooted in the Japanese tradition, studied composition in America during the 1950s and became one of the first leaders of the movement towards a synthesis in the 1960s. While Yuize set music for traditional instruments based on new instrumental groupings and compositional techniques derived from the West, others went for a different form of combination – settings for the instruments of the Western orchestra of music composed in the traditional Japanese pattern.

Of course, a field such as this offered much scope for abuse and banal pastiche. There are innumerable LP versions of pieces like *Variations on*

Above
*Yuize Shin'ichi,
one of a great
family of musicians,
plays the* samisen
*at a public concert
in Nagano.*

Below
*Yuize is also a
master of the* koto,
*an instrument
still very popular
with young women
because of its value
as a passport to
a good marriage.*

the Cherry Blossom Theme (Sakura – Cherry Blossom–is a favourite old song) set for the big band and cascading strings that were so characteristic of the 1950s in the West. But there are significant and serious compositions around Japanese themes for Western orchestral ensembles by such men as Takemitsu Tōru or Mayuzumi Toshirō. Many talented newcomers follow where these led: the works of nineteen Japanese composers were heard at a recent festival in Paris. Again, there has been a steady increase in the number of Japanese soloists of international standing and many Western orchestras have Japanese string players.

The Japanese writers and people of the arts whose name became household words in the West during the 1960s had often rooted their skills firmly in the soil of the tradition and it was this that lent part of its distinctive strength to their creations. The style of Kawabata Yasunari, winner of the Nobel Prize for Literature in 1968, for instance, often draws heavily on the Japanese tradition. The structure of his works is sometimes reminiscent of the prose-poem mix of the tenth century, or of seventeenth century *haiku,* and he often wrote in the typical Japanese mood of gentle melancholy, and in forms governed by the old lyricism. As did the *haiku* poets, Kawabata often links opposite images, or mingles the senses, giving colour to a sound. (Bashō had called the flight of teal

Left and right
*Two of the
buildings in
Tokyo designed
by Tange Kenzō –
the National
Stadium and the
Roman Catholic
Cathedral.*

'palely white'.) So, in *Snow Country*, there is the 'roaring silence of a winter night', or the 'brightness of snow burning icily'. There is also the 'sound of the freezing snow roaring deep into the earth'. In fact, the novel as a whole has a *haikai* (linked verse) structure – a series of brief flashes, contrasting yet culminating in a confirmation or resolution which is hinted – but not expressly stated – in best traditional style.

Tange Kenzō, architect of the National Stadium built for the Tokyo Olympics in 1964, is another whose work links back to the tradition. The line of the roof of the National Stadium is reminiscent of that of a *torii* (the gateway to a Shintō shrine). Tange's treatment of concrete is also peculiarly Japanese. Both in the National Stadium and in St Mary's Church (another of the buildings in Tokyo which he designed), the angles are not those of Western design; they are softer and not based on the assumptions of European architecture. Planes are not linked on a perpendicular or ninety degree relationship and, as a result, there is a sensation of flow or welling up of 'feeling' and emotion in a Tange concrete surface which the sheer angular symmetry of a western structure would not permit. (This sensation is related to that of the undulation and the curve of the moss base of the Moss Temple, which would not be possible with a close-clipped lawn base.)

The skills of Mishima Yukio too, writer and playwright, derived in some measure from the synthesis of the 1960s. Certainly, his work was rooted in the tradition. He created a group of modern *Nō* plays, in which he took a traditional play and adapted it to plots and settings based on the late nineteenth or mid-twentieth century. (*Nō* drama had been used before by modernisers or synthesisers: soon after the Meiji Restoration, when the thoughts of Samuel Smiles in *Self Help* were in great vogue as a testament for the New Japan, there appeared a version in this traditional dramatic form.)

Although he did not let himself live to feel it, Mishima was really a man in sympathy with the spirit of the 1970s. For the 1970s saw a move back behind the synthesis of the previous years to a greater appreciation of traditional values. The spirit of the new decade is perhaps best symbolised by the tragic drama of Mishima's suicide by ritual disembowelment – the death of the *samurai* – late in 1970. Part of his motive was to urge his fellow Japanese to return to and respect their traditions.

Earlier in the same year we had been working together on an anthology of new Japanese writing, in both traditional and modern forms. He was equally at home in both, and, while he knew his own classics better than any Japanese I have known, yet he was fully familiar with the whole range of contemporary literature. He had talked quite dispassionately about the threat that the Japanese themselves were posing to indigenous values – a threat he sensed was more insidious than any ever levelled before at Japanese culture, either by China or by the West in the Meiji period. Yet, almost in the same breath, he went on to discuss the prospects for the survival of the tradition. 'Let us only retain the tea ceremony', he argued, 'and with it we shall preserve so many aspects of our indigenous artistic experience. In architecture, for instance, the traditional tea house and that distinctive sense of unity between natural and man-made – garden and house; the skills of potter, lacquer and bamboo craftsman; artist – painter and calligrapher – for the alcove scroll; master of flower arrangement and weaver and silk craftsman for *kimono*.'

Mishima's sympathy for – and his skill in manipulating – the tradition is best indicated in his attempt sometimes in prose to reproduce one of the artifices of the urbane Heian period poet. The poet would so mix Chinese character and simpler Japanese syllabic symbol (*kana*) as to create a pattern aesthetically pleasing to the eye. Where he had written with such care and precision, Mishima used to ensure that the printer faithfully followed the manuscript line-length, so as to preserve his exquisitely plotted pattern. (How, incidentally, can a translator do justice to such craft?)

Mishima was not alone in his faith in traditional values. It is as if the Japanese need to recharge their batteries with power from their own traditions; this Japanese power then engenders a self-assurance and a confidence in their ability which helps to explain the growing appeal of indigenous values during the 1970s.

Traditional elements in contemporary culture

The spirit of the traditional survives today in many aspects of contemporary culture, in the 'meeting of feeling' that still marks the mutual and intuitive grasp of an emotion or mood in another. Nō drama survives, as a sort of museum piece, without any additions to the corpus; it is subsidised and relies on the enthusiasm of a restricted number of devotees. Today's Nō scene epitomises the octopus-pot society theory: each group tends to be confined in its own pot, and has few links with the others – so that with five schools of Nō drama alive today, some of the repertory is exclusive to one of the five, which jealously guards traditions of performance and so on, and audiences become attached to one school to the exclusion of the others.

Kabuki, originally the theatre of the bourgeoisie, has a wider following. The corpus has grown, with recent additions to the traditional repertoire. Actors have enthusiastic groups of followers, and there are many young people who track the rise of a new star or take a deep interest in experimental *kabuki*. But, of course, at performances of traditional plays there is always a high percentage of grandmothers, tissues (a good Japanese tradition, known in the eleventh century) or handkerchiefs at the ready. (The really 'good' *kabuki* play is one that will require seven – I think it is – handkerchiefs.) Again, *kabuki* lives on not just in the theatre but, in a sense, as the essence of all the novels set in the *samurai* period which are based on dramas first enacted on or rewritten for the *kabuki* stage. *Kabuki*, too, makes fine television – either the real thing put on screen or, again as with the novel, as the basis of rollicking 'Wild-East' drama. In the same way, *kabuki* lives on in the film. In a sense, with its techniques such as wipes and cuts, *kabuki* was film; the *emakimono* – a long picture scroll, with successive frames, slightly different, adding to the descriptive background or the action – was Japanese film created in the twelfth century. The first ten minutes of Kinugasa's *Gate of Hell* (which won a Venice prize early in the 1950s) used the colours, the subjects, and the techniques of the *emakimono* painter.

Side by side with these traditional styles, there are modern forms of Japanese theatre which are now almost traditional (they arrived with the new age of the Meiji period), there are performances of the masterpieces of the West in translation and there is underground theatre.

Traditional co-exists with modern, indigenous with alien, in just the same way in the world of poetry. Both *tanka* and *haiku* forms survive lustily. The Emperor's New Year poetry contest draws thousands of *tanka* entries each year, there are *haiku* clubs in any town with cultural pretensions, each of them producing its cyclostyled monthly, and nearly all the major publishers have a sizeable list of contemporary *haiku* or *tanka* poets. As with *kabuki*, the traditions of the *tanka* poet live on, a thousand years after, in other contexts. A good many current and contemporary tunes in the old mould (not 'pop' as it would now be understood, but songs in the traditional popular style) have lyrics which echo faithfully the mood in which the Heian poet composed and the metre he used (an alternation of lines of five and seven syllables), and even dwell on the same aspects of the world of nature about him! The dominant theme is sentimental – there are partings, memories (sad), regrets, and loneliness; 'love' is not active but the pining melancholy after parting. As with *tanka* and *haiku*, the singer expresses feeling not by direct relational expressions or personal pronouns, but by allusive and indirect natural descriptions – 'rain is crying this lonely evening' or 'a heart is wet under the moonlight'. The wind, the rain and mist are the most common references to the natural world, and cry, part, think of, pass by, and wait, are the most regular verbs. The most frequently used syllable is 'oh!'

Parallel with the surviving tradition in the world of poetry there is the 'new-style' poem – in which there is a freedom of diction and form not permitted by the traditional styles. This new style originated with a selection of translations from Western poetry in 1882 (including Tennyson, Gray's Elegy, and excerpts from *Hamlet*) together with originals such as *The Principles of Sociology* from Japanese brushes. Since then, 'new-style' poetry in Japan has followed nearly all the vogues of Western fashion. In the 1920s, for instance, there were Dadaism, Cubism, and Surrealism, proletarian and anarchist poets. Soon after the War, Eliot's *The Waste Land* hit the Japanese hard, and one of the leading groups today is still the *Arechi* (*Waste Land*) School.

Some of the serious (often priestly) polite arts of the medieval period survive today as pastimes or hobbies – though there is often a deep commitment to such pastimes in women of marriageable age, since they are widely regarded as socially desirable accomplishments and may well therefore lead to a better match. A recent survey of hobbies and forms of relaxation in Japan showed that over seventeen per cent of women learn flower arrangement and more than six per cent the tea ceremony (with peak popularity for these pastimes in the twenty to twenty-four age group, on the threshold of marriage – when thirty-four per cent take up flower arrangement and sixteen per cent the tea ceremony). As with *Nō* and other traditional cultural forms, there is a number of competing schools, each with its own singular canon.

There is a wide range of musical activities in contemporary Japan. Alongside developments in composition and performance, there is still a lively interest in purely traditional music (*koto* and *samisen* – plucked

Above and below Two of the polite arts of the medieval period which still survive as serious pastimes – Ikebana, *flower arranging, and* Chanoyu, *the tea ceremony.*

Left
*Kurosawa's
Rashōmon,
which won the
Grand Prix at the
Venice Film
Festival of 1951.*

Above
*Kurosawa's
Throne of Blood,
a version of
'Macbeth', with
the hero as a
sixteenth century
Japanese warlord.*

strings, and the various flute forms, *shakuhachi* and *fue*). Accomplishment
in one of the stringed instruments is another form of passport to a better
marriage and the playing of a musical instrument reaches its highest
figure (thirty per cent) among women in their twenties. There is an ever-
increasing vogue for Western music of every kind, from grand opera
through orchestral and instrumental classical music to pop. Tokyo alone
has nine orchestras, there are modern concert halls in all the major cities,
and it has been said that Japan alone accounts for half the world sales of
Karajan's records. I remember failing to find a mono recording, even as
early as 1960, of the Choral Symphony; meanwhile, there were any
number of recordings of all Beethoven's symphonies in stereo. Today,
over half of Japan's thirty-four million households possess stereo equipment. Nor are the Japanese merely idle listeners – twelve per cent of
households have a piano and twenty-three per cent an electric organ,
which means something like eight million organs. The cinema was the
first of Japan's arts to gain international recognition after the War.
Indeed, although the West came to know it after *Rashōmon* took the
Venice Grand Prix in 1951, the Japanese film is as old as the cinema itself.
Much of the mood and some of the basic techniques of Japan's twentieth
century directors come from the traditional arts. Ichikawa (*The Olympiad*
and *Tale of Genji*) discovers in his subjects and scenes a melancholy beauty

Above
Kinugasa's Gate of
Hell, *the story of
a twelfth century
soldier who demands
a married woman
as his prize.*

Centre
Tokyo Story, *one of
Ōzu's most moving
films about family
relationships.*

Below
Ōshima's Diary
of a Shinjuku
Thief, *a film about
a young man
who steals books,
and his sexual
problems.*

The Life of Oharu, *one of Mizoguchi's many films about prostitutes, based on a seventeenth century story.*

(the *aware* of medieval literature). Mizoguchi's vignettes are reminiscent of episodic literary genres, and Kinugasa (who was an *onnagata* – player of female parts in *kabuki*) with his use of colour recalls a scroll or print (*Gate of Hell*). Kurosawa is at home in all styles – his vivid treatment of contemporary social issues (*Ikiru*), for instance, or his transition as in a Nō play between illusion and reality (*Rashomon*). Ozu's favourite theme is the old-style Japanese family (*Tokyo Monogatari*). Of the new names, Ōshima Nagisa, the centre of the New Wave, attacks established values (*Diary of a Shinjuku Thief*). It is sad that television and pornography have dealt so cruelly with figures of the international stature of Kurosawa and Ichikawa. However, there are very recent indications that the old masters are regaining their stature in the eyes of the Japanese public, and that there are assured domestic outlets for their talents.

Conclusion

I have tried to indicate how the tradition of Japanese culture has grown, how it forms a continuity, with no sudden breaks with the past, and how new elements are incorporated, to enhance the corpus. Will these cultural processes of the past persist into the future?

I have a firm confidence in the tenacity of Japanese values. Many observers, both Japanese and foreign, have sensed a renewed appreciation of the indigenous culture, growing with the 1970s. This has led the Japanese to question the destruction of their rich natural environment, the savage competition between group and group, man and man, and other products of the years of swift economic growth.

Again, as more than once in the past, contact with the alien and the subsequent return to loyalty to the traditional canon has generated a creativity and a confidence – sometimes over-cocky – in a variety of sectors, the technological as well as the cultural.

During the 1980s the Japanese may give a freer rein to his individuality. This, in turn, may quicken a fertility distinctively – and sometimes insensitively – Japanese.

Above
Satō Taikan,
a famous painter
and calligrapher,
working in black
ink (Sumi-e).

Below
Nō *drama.*
Princess Rokujō,
transformed
by her jealousy
into a demon,
tries to revenge
herself on her
former lover.

4
Economic growth
and industrial competition

Douglas Anthony

Introduction

In less than a hundred years Japan has been transformed from a predominantly agricultural into an urban, industrial society. This transformation was a deliberate act of national policy. The leaders of the Meiji revolution of 1868 were intent on the creation of a modern state, and modernisation the world over was known to accompany, indeed to be almost synonymous with, industrialisation. Yet Japan has few of the raw materials necessary for modern industry; and she was unable to attract enough foreign capital fast enough to influence the speed of her industrialisation. She had, therefore, to find ways of mobilising her own savings and directing them into the hands of those willing to invest in new methods of production, especially those which could earn the foreign exchange to purchase both the raw materials and the new technology necessary for the development of Japanese industry.

In the Meiji period (1868–1912), when Japan was a predominantly agricultural nation, these savings came largely from a land tax which provided most of the Government's revenue. With this revenue, the Government set about creating the institutions and the infrastructure of a modern state; it also encouraged the creation of modern industries. By the 1930s a pattern of production and trade had developed in which Japan exported the products of her traditional industries (silk thread, tea, etc.) to earn the foreign exchange to buy the raw materials for her consumer goods industries – notably raw cotton for the textile industry. Her textiles were then sold in the Asian market in return for the raw materials – like oil – for her heavy industries. The products of these industries – like chemicals and machinery – were sold in the protected markets of her colonies (Formosa, Korea, and – though it was never

Lanterns in the trees in Tokyo's Ueno Park, a favourite place for cherry blossom viewing.

127

completely colonised – China); and in exchange Japan imported basic foodstuffs like rice and raw materials like coal and iron ore.

Another important feature of the pre-war economy was the appearance of the *zaibatsu*. During the 1920s and 1930s Japanese industry had become so large that it could no longer be financed from the savings of individuals or the revenue obtained from taxing farmers. Corporate savings from the profits of the small number of large, modern enterprises were therefore vitally important for the expansion of existing industries and for establishing new ones. The result was the establishment of groups of firms where control was centralised in the hands of the top management, or in the hands of a single family who in part constituted the management. Between them, these powerful groups – the *zaibatsu* – dominated almost every field of large-scale industry, commerce and finance, and competition among these groups gave a characteristic dynamism to Japan's industrial expansion.

The Second World War shattered the precarious balance of the Japanese economy. Apart from the death and destruction caused by bombing, the scrapping of machinery which had been used to make munitions, and the embargo put on the use of some of the country's industrial capacity, Japan also lost her colonies – Korea, Formosa and the parts of China which had been under her control. In addition, the allied occupying powers were not originally concerned with Japan's economic recovery, but only with democratising some of her institutions and certain sectors of her economy. (To all intents and purposes 'the allied occupying powers' meant the United States under the title of Supreme Commander for the Allied Powers (SCAP), which referred both to General Douglas MacArthur and to his administration.) Indeed, SCAP's early policy also had a punitive element, which is well illustrated by the plan, never fully implemented and later dropped, to dismantle a sizeable part of Japan's industrial machinery and ship it off as reparation to those countries which had suffered most at Japan's hands during the war. It was in the democratising spirit that SCAP carried through a major reform of land ownership and trade union law, and broke up the *zaibatsu*. The shares in the firms constituting these groups which were held by the controlling families or managers were first confiscated and then dispersed; senior managers were purged from business life, and a considerable number of firms were dissolved or dismembered. In 1947 a stringent anti-monopoly law was also passed, designed partly to make it much less easy for so many of Japan's industries to be dominated by a few large firms. But Japan was still an urban, industrial nation with the over-riding need to sell her products in world markets. She was, however, doubly debarred from competing successfully in these markets. Much of her industrial capacity had been destroyed and her traditional markets were closed to her. She also had to come to terms with a new legal

The Mitsubishi Heavy Industries shipyard at Kobe. In the mid-1970's the yard could produce 700,000 tons of shipping a year

framework and new institutions, and she needed time for a new generation of industrial leaders to find their feet. In spite of these considerable disadvantages Japan's economic development during the next twenty-five years was to be the most spectacular in her history.

Postwar economic growth – the beginnings

SCAP had soon realised that democracy would not flourish where economic survival was a hand-to-mouth business. The immediate post-war years of hardship, shortage, and stern-faced American policies gave way therefore in the late 1940s to a fragile sufficiency, based mainly on American aid and accompanied by less punitive policies. Economic aid from the United States, which reached a peak of 535 million dollars in 1949, was, however, soon exceeded by American military expenditure in Japan as a result of the Korean War; in 1952, and again in 1953, this was well over 800 million dollars. This windfall did a great deal to introduce a new era of prosperity for Japan's industry.

The skyscrapers at Shinjuku — a well-known Tokyo landmark.

In the meantime, the end of the occupation in 1952 allowed the Japanese Government to make certain modifications to the policies introduced by SCAP, and especially to the anti-monopoly law of 1947. In particular this meant the reconstitution of firms into the groups that were to characterise large-scale industry in the 1960s and 1970s. Some firms which had been dissolved were re-established, and some purged leaders re-entered business life. Most important of all, the banks, which had figured so prominently in *zaibatsu* activities before the Second World War, had escaped the reforming zeal of the occupying authorities bent on breaking down concentrations of economic power. They were therefore able to play the most important role in financing the economic expansion which began in the late 1950s.

The financing of rapid economic growth

By 1953 both industrial production and national income had reached pre-war levels. Between 1953 and 1973 Japan's economic growth averaged about ten per cent a year, much faster than other industrial nations, either in the West or in Eastern Europe. One notable feature of this period of astonishing economic expansion is that the Japanese have continuously devoted much of their efforts not to producing goods for immediate consumption, but to producing machines and equipment (capital goods) whose purpose is to increase the output of consumer goods in the future. Moreover Japan, far more than most countries, has concentrated its investment in the advanced manufacturing sectors of industry, such as steel and chemicals, where – because of the effects of economies of scale – the returns on investment are relatively high. This investment in new capital equipment, which has been greater than in any country outside the centrally-controlled economies of Eastern Europe, has been primarily the achievement not of the Government, but of private industry.

The investment has also been financed largely out of private savings. This is partly because incomes have risen so fast. But over the last century or more the Japanese have always tended to save a large proportion of their incomes, even when these were not increasing quickly, and this has been true even of the less prosperous. Traditional habits of thrift, the necessity for precautionary savings amongst the very large number of small farmers, tradesmen and businessmen, and the high proportion of their income which Japanese wage- and salary-earners receive as a lump-sum in the form of twice yearly bonuses, are all factors which have encouraged high rates of private saving. The absence of a thoroughgoing

Television sets
being assembled
at the Ibaragi
plant of Matsushita
Electrical in 1964.
The notice says
'The next stage is
the consumer.
Let's make sure he
gets satisfactory
quality'.

state welfare service also makes private saving a greater necessity than in other countries; so too does the high cost to the family of education in a country where higher education has increasingly become the only passport to economic security.

The Edobashi interchange on the Tokyo urban motorway system.

The pattern of saving in Japan helps to explain how high levels of investment, and consequently such rapid economic growth, have been financed. The average wage- or salary-earner, as well as many small businessmen, puts his savings into a bank deposit account. There are several reasons for this. Firstly, bank deposit income is taxed at a lower rate than other forms of income from assets (for example, dividends). Secondly, the fact that savings are made partly for emergencies (like sickness or unemployment), which are not well provided for by the state,

makes it important that they should be easily accessible, and bank deposits are the obvious form. Thirdly, the consumer credit industry only began to develop on any scale in the 1970s. Before that, saving with a bank was the normal way in which families got together enough money to buy the consumer durables that crowd Japanese houses.

The result is that in the last thirty years there has been a large and steady flow of private savings into Japanese banks. Lending to industry, either for investment or for working capital, is by far the most important function, and source of revenue, of commercial banks in Japan. The important part played by the banks in providing capital is reflected in the capital structure of Japanese companies. There has been much less reliance on internal sources of finance (retained surpluses and depreciation allowances) in Japan than elsewhere in the free-enterprise, industrial world, although there are signs that this may now be changing. Nor have firms gone so readily to the stock market to raise funds. Instead Japanese companies, particularly the larger ones, have borrowed from the commercial banks on a scale unknown elsewhere. This has meant that the ratio of share capital to total capital is markedly lower in Japan than in the United Kingdom, the United States, or Germany; and, in addition, that the ratio of loans from banks to the total capital of Japanese companies has been exceptionally high.

This was not the case in pre-war Japan. The main reason for the change after the War is clearly connected with the fact that the banks were left untouched by the anti-concentration measures of the occupying authorities. This, together with the strong inflow of funds from private savers, put the banks in a position to supply the financial needs of a growing industry in the second half of the 1950s when other sources of finance were simply not available. Competition amongst the banks to lend to industry was so fierce indeed that between 1955 and 1961 the thirteen major banks increased their annual loans two or three times.

It was therefore during this period that the banks came to achieve their key position in the Japanese economy. To meet industry's voracious demand for finance Japan's banks continuously held their liquid assets ratio (the ratio of loans to deposits and other assets) at a level which would be regarded as dangerously high by the rules of sound banking practice outside Japan. The banks were able to do this since the Bank of Japan in turn lent them money whenever they appeared to be extending themselves too far. In this way the Government, through its central bank, has been a partner in a process which guaranteed the supply of low interest finance to industry. Some writers have argued, unconvincingly in my opinion, that the Bank of Japan was very reluctant to underwrite the banks' precarious liquid assets ratio. I believe that, once the effectiveness of the system had been demonstrated, there were only token noises of disapproval from official sources.

About two-thirds of the loans made by the commercial banks have been made to the larger industrial firms which have grown faster. There is a great deal of evidence to show that banks have lent more cheaply to these larger firms (where the risk involved is generally less) than when lending to small firms. It has been estimated in one study, for example, that, during the period of rapid growth from the mid-1950s to the early 1970s, the largest class of firms (those with paid-up capital of 1,000 million yen or more) paid a third less for their borrowings than smaller firms (those with less than 100 million yen paid-up capital). Indeed, access to bank loans has been restricted for smaller firms, which has led to the development of different, though as yet not fully satisfactory, credit arrangements and institutions for them. The system has also given the commercial banks a much larger say in the decision-making processes of Japanese industry than is common elsewhere. Nevertheless, as a way of financing economic growth at an unprecedented rate, it must be regarded as highly successful.

The body assembly line at the Tochigi plant of Nissan, the largest of the company's five plants.

Economic growth and the supply of labour

Japan has often been regarded as a country where the speed of economic growth has never been held back by a shortage of labour. However, Japan's population has only grown by a little over one per cent a year since the war, whilst during the same period the labour force increased by a little under one and-a-half per cent a year. Neither rate is significantly different from other industrialised countries. At the same time we know that during this period *fewer* people have actually become available for employment, mainly because of an increase in the number of young people going on into higher education. We also know that the average number of hours worked, while still high by the standards of other industrial countries, has gradually fallen over the last ten years with the slow extension of the five-day working week. Finally, until very recently, unemployment in Japan has been very low.

In what sense, then, has Japan never been short of labour? The idea can only make sense if it means that the advanced, large-scale manufacturing sector of industry has always been able to attract enough good labour at wages which have still preserved both the high level of its profits and its strong urge to invest. But at the same time this sector, whilst it has been responsible for the bulk of the investment which fuelled economic growth, is one where a great deal of capital is employed and relatively little labour. (The low manning levels in the Japanese steel and motor car industries, for example, have received a good deal of publicity in the West.) There must therefore be parts of the economy where great numbers of people are employed, using production techniques which rely much less on high levels of capital expenditure. One

of these areas is agriculture; another is those sectors of industry, commerce and services where there are very large numbers of small firms.

Agriculture

In the early post-war years agriculture was a very large employer of labour; in the years 1953 to 1955, for example, nearly forty per cent of the labour force was engaged in agriculture. By the early 1970s, this proportion had fallen below fifteen per cent; by 1977 slightly more than eleven per cent of the working population was engaged in agriculture and the decline still continues. The Land Reform Act of 1947 had the effect of establishing the small-scale owner-farmer in a virtually impregnable position. In addition, the low prices at which transfers of land were made under the Act, together with the sharp fall in their expenses now that rents no longer had to be paid, raised farmers' incomes. This in turn provided a much-needed increase in the demand for the products of Japan's industries.

Stimulated by the parallel increase in demand for food from an urban population growing steadily larger and better-off, farmers worked hard to raise output. This was achieved largely through the ever more intensive use of chemical fertilisers, while in more recent years machines have

been increasingly used to supplement the efforts of the declining labour force. Small, versatile hand-tractors, well-suited to the cultivation of paddy land, relatively inexpensive and so well within the means of Japan's multitude of small farmers, have been important here. Nevertheless, agricultural productivity increased relatively slowly and, with the exception of rice, production was unable to keep up with the increase in the demand for food.

As a result of this relatively slow growth in agricultural productivity, incomes in rural areas failed to keep pace with those of urban workers. This increased the lure of the city for farmers and farmworkers, who were already becoming aware of the pleasures of city life as television sets found their way into almost every farmhouse. Farmers' sons left the land to work in the towns and cities, whilst farmers themselves, in ever-increasing numbers, chose to supplement their incomes by taking other jobs. Some commute to nearby towns and farm only at weekends and on public holidays; others have joined the migratory labour force, which works in engineering and construction and in small industries, only returning to the farm at harvest time and for the transplanting of the young rice. The result has been that many Japanese farms are now run by women – the mothers, wives and daughters of the farmers. Recent figures suggest, in fact, that those who work wholly or mainly on the land only slightly outnumber those who farm part-time but work mainly at other jobs. While it would be wrong to say that this has led to

Mechanisation of Japan's agriculture. Even farmers with a little land frequently use machines like this to plant their rice crop.

a general lowering of farming standards, it is difficult to see that there can be any marked increases in productivity in the future without a radical restructuring of Japanese agriculture. As yet there are no signs that this will take place.

The way in which agriculture has developed since the war has therefore contributed to the process of rapid industrialisation. A young man who has been brought up on a farm and who decides to make his career in a city, however, would not normally expect to be employed by one of the large, technically advanced firms in manufacturing, commerce or finance. He is more likely to find a job in one of the many medium and small enterprises which are such an important feature of Japan's industry. 'Medium and small enterprises' is a literal translation of the common Japanese term *chūsho kigyō*. Its legal definition is an enterprise with less than 300 employees in manufacturing, less than 100 employees in wholesaling or less than fifty employees in retailing and the service trades. It is firms such as these which are the other great employers of labour in Japan.

Medium and small enterprises

There are a great many such firms – more than 5,358,000 in 1975, which is substantially more than in any other industrial country. There are 800,000 in manufacturing alone. In addition, these establishments employ eighty per cent of all industrial workers, which is more than double the proportion of those employed in similar firms in either the United States or the United Kingdom. (A comparison with countries such as France and Italy, on the other hand, would show much closer figures for the proportion of the workforce employed in small firms, although differences of definition and statistical difficulties make really accurate figures hard to come by.) Even more significant perhaps is the fact that, in Japan, very small firms, with less than fifty employees, account for approximately thirty-five per cent of the industrial workforce. Small firms the world over have certain features in common, such as the blurring of the distinction between management and workers, a less bureaucratic structure, whole families working together side by side, and so on; Japan is no exception. But in addition, there are several features of small firms in Japan which mark them off very distinctly from large firms.

Firstly, these small firms often have a precarious existence. In 1977, 18,741 companies went bankrupt, and the overwhelming majority were small firms. Small firms do not have the ready access to bank loans that large firms do. As a result they rely heavily on their current earnings both to finance their operations and to invest in new plant and machinery, and their reserves are low. The Government has done something to help by sponsoring semi-governmental financial institutions to provide capital to small firms so that they can plan their operations over a longer period. There are also several private institutions which provide finance for small firms. Except during periods of extreme buoyancy in the economy, however, the supply of capital is still inadequate and at other times many small firms find it virtually impossible to raise money.

A tempting way around this problem for the small firm is to ally itself with a large firm which has ready access to finance. Large manufacturing firms in Japan frequently sub-contract work to small firms which in the United Kingdom would be part of their own operations. The main advantages in this arrangement for the small firm are access to credit to finance its operations and a steady outlet for its products. The advantage to the large firm is that by sub-contracting to several small firms it can force down their prices by encouraging competition amongst them for its orders. There is also some evidence to show that in times of recession additional pressure is brought to bear to lower these prices, and therefore its own costs, still further. As a result, the large firm can continue both to employ its high-cost workforce and to keep its expensive capital equipment operating, whilst it passes on much of the burden of declining demand to the small firms who operate as its sub-contractors. In more recent years, this feature of the relationship between small and large firms has changed somewhat. With increasing competition, larger firms have begun to demand higher standards from their sub-contractors. Many have also taken large shareholdings in the small firms with which they deal. These factors have combined to make the large firm less predatory in its dealings with its smaller customers.

The position of workers in small businesses is equally precarious; not for them the guarantee of life-time employment or the welcome fringe benefits enjoyed by the employees of a large company. These include subsidised housing, medical care, and pension schemes, as well as access to the company's sports facilities in a sports-minded nation where public facilities are seriously inadequate. Similarly, few workers in small businesses belong to trades unions, and there has been little attempt to organise them. This has meant that many of these workers have received less than their fair share of Japan's growing prosperity. The absence in Japan of much of the state provision for social welfare which has become common in the West has also meant that the fear of illness, injury, unemployment, and old age, is a major – and entirely justified – preoccupation of workers in small businesses. Most of the under-privileged in Japanese society are workers in such firms.

Another important reason why real earnings in small firms are lower than in large firms is that productivity is lower, which reflects the fact that small firms have inferior plant and machinery. Reliable indices of real earnings, which include the value of fringe benefits, are impossible to come by. In 1975, however, cash wages per employee averaged 1,382,000 yen in firms with under 300 employees, and 2,328,000 yen for workers in firms with more than 300 employees. (At early 1980 rates of exchange these figures were £2,513 and £4,232 respectively.)

Small firms have therefore acted first of all as a reserve pool of potential labour for large firms, and also as a source of employment for those leaving the countryside for the cities. The result has been that both large and small firms have been able to supply their additional needs for labour comparatively cheaply. This in turn has kept down increases in both wages and prices, and helped to create the international competitiveness of Japanese industry. The flexibility of small firms has also enabled them to use labour-intensive methods at times when labour was easily available, while still allowing them to adopt more capital-intensive methods when labour was in short supply. They have done this by importing foreign technology, by adapting techniques developed by large firms, and by using their discarded machines and equipment.

These then are the main reasons why the growth in productivity exceeded that of real wages by an estimated one to one-and-a-half per cent a year between 1953 and 1973. This in turn allowed companies to build up surpluses out of which they could finance new investment, and led to the relatively low prices of Japan's goods in international markets. There are, I believe, two other reasons for this. The first is that – in large companies – company unions have encouraged the feeling that the interests of the worker and that of the firm were very close. This has meant that wage claims were not pressed as hard as they might have been, even when a shortage of labour gave the unions a strong bargaining position. A second and related reason is that, in my opinion, there has been an unwritten contract between the Japanese worker on the one hand, and the employers in large firms and the Government on the other. The terms of this contract are that, in return for the national prestige conferred by the economic miracle, wage claims will be moderate. But the observance of this contract and the predominance of the company union have meant that the unions are now unable to resist the latest argument from employers that recession and slow growth must be countered by wage claims which continue to be 'moderate' (that is, less than the measured increases in the productivity of labour). Economic growth in Japan has been achieved, in fact, as the result of a system which contains large elements of exploitation and injustice.

Competition in Japanese industry – small firms

As we have seen, there are an extremely large number of small firms in Japanese industry. For example, in the services industry more than ninety-eight per cent of establishments have less than fifty employees,

and they employ about seventy per cent of the total workforce in this sector. In the retail sector, too, over ninety-nine per cent of establishments are equally small. They employ roughly ninety per cent of the workers in retail businesses and account for about eighty per cent of total sales. In wholesaling, ninety-nine per cent of establishments have less than a hundred employees, employ eighty per cent of the workforce in this sector and account for roughly fifty-five per cent of sales. Because of the large number of firms in these sectors the share of each in the total

A corner Oden *stall in the Hatchobori district of Tokyo – Japan's version of the fast foodstore.*

demand for their products is generally small, prices – and consequently profits – are low, and the penalty for the failure to satisfy customers as cheaply as their rivals is swift and cruel. In addition, Japanese consumers have clung rather more tenaciously than those in other industrialised nations to more 'traditional' habits of consumption. This is particularly so in the case of food. It is also true to a large extent of the way houses are furnished and decorated. This has meant that small firms producing 'traditional' goods – like the *tatami* maker (the rush matting for the floors of Japanese houses) – have been able to survive in large numbers.

Large firms do of course exist in all these sectors, but they are only significant in small areas of the services sector, such as insurance. In retailing, the establishment of local branches in recent years by supermarket chains and department stores has introduced a new element of competition in this sector; but, so far, the consumer appears to have been the main beneficiary as small shops have fought to hold their own. They have largely succeeded, but at some cost to themselves, by their willingness to tolerate very long opening hours, poor living accommodation (frequently on the premises), and lagging real incomes in order to survive. The visitor to Japan is often surprised to find local shops of such a variety and in such numbers. He is also surprised that they stay open until about 9 pm and sometimes later, and that many still open seven days a week.

In manufacturing, the position of the small firm is somewhat more complicated. The 1974 Census of Manufacturers identifies 532 manufacturing industries in Japan. Over ninety-nine per cent of the establishments, roughly seventy per cent of the employees and about fifty-one per cent of total sales are accounted for by small firms. 324 industries are dominated by small firms which are responsible for seventy per cent or more of total sales. Competition in these industries is therefore fierce, and profits are generally low.

In 137 industries large and small firms co-exist, with neither type predominant. It is difficult to generalise about the nature of competition in these industries, although one suspects that in many of them prices are fixed by a small number of large firms. The remaining – and relatively large – number of small firms then compete for their share of the market by supplying what they can at that price. The situation is complicated by the fact that much sub-contracting goes on in these industries, so that large firms have a powerful hand in determining the prices of the products of small firms because of their position as powerful buyers in a market of small, competing sellers.

The remaining seventy-one industries were dominated by large firms. These are industries where a very small number of firms producing on a large scale compete with each other in domestic and international markets. They produce the mass consumer durables such as television

sets and cars, or they supply the steel, chemicals, and other vital inter-
mediate products for these industries.

Large firms

The behaviour of the few large firms in Japanese industry is determined
by a policy which emphasises a rapid growth in sales as the best way of
protecting each firm's share of the market, and hence its long-term
viability. Rapid investment in the newest technology, usually accompanied by mass-production, was the main feature of this kind of competition throughout the period of rapid economic growth. In many
industries the large domestic market was first saturated; the economies
of scale and the high productivity achieved in the process subsequently
allowed Japanese firms to capture international markets through a
combination of low prices and high quality goods. But this process was
accompanied by a parallel development – the formation of powerful
groups of enterprises. Within these groups the member firms appear
ready to sacrifice a certain degree of independence in the decision-making
process in return for the benefits of belonging to the group.

In order to understand the nature of these benefits we must once again
go back to the early years of rapid economic growth which began in the
late 1950s. At this time there were many profitable opportunities for
investment. New technologies, like synthetic fibres, generally developed
in North America or Western Europe, were becoming available relatively
cheaply to the Japanese. The rate at which the economy was expanding
also meant that there was room for greater capacity in such basic industries as iron and steel, chemicals, paper and some of the consumer
durables, such as cars and refrigerators. In this way, industries which
had formerly been dominated by a very small number of firms, like
paper and iron and steel, and new industries, like synthetic fibres and
refrigerators, all became much more competitive. There was an increase
in the number of firms making these products and the potential rewards
for enterprise were considerable.

We saw earlier that the sources of new finance were extremely limited,
since for all practical purposes they were confined to the thirteen major
banks, backed by the Bank of Japan. Although it is not absolutely clear
why, it appears that at this point the traditions of the pre-war period
reasserted themselves. In the rush to enter the new and the growing
fields of industry, Mitsubishi Bank appears to have given preference to
firms who belonged to, or were connected with, the pre-war and wartime
Mitsubishi financial empires (*zaibatsu*) in the granting of loans. Both
Mitsui Bank and Sumitomo Bank did the same; and so also did the Fuji
Bank, which was the post-war successor to the main financial organ of
the Yasuda *zaibatsu*. Similar groups of firms gathered around the Dai-

Above
*One of the large
shipyards which,
during the 1960's
and early 1970's,
were powerful
symbols of Japan's
economic miracle.
And below,
a smaller shipyard
which weathered the
severe recession
of the later 1970's.*

ichi Kangyō Bank and the Sanwa Bank. This was the reason for the establishment of the six great groups, or *keiretsu*, which have been a major feature of the post-war Japanese economy.

Relations within the *keiretsu*

Although there were variations between these groups, it was commonly the case in the late 1950s and early 1960s that a firm belonging to a group would obtain between thirty and forty per cent of its loans from one or other of the group's financial organisations, with the group's bank as the major source of supply. By the middle of the 1970s, the proportion was more commonly twenty to thirty per cent, which indicates something of a weakening of the hold the group bank had over the financial purse strings of group firms. The sheer pace of expansion has meant that firms have had to go outside the group, chiefly to long-term trust banks and Government or semi-governmental financial institutions, to supply their needs for new investment finance. But firms within one group still have relatively little recourse to the banks of another group; less than five per cent of their borrowing requirements are usually supplied in this way.

In the 1970s firms belonging to the six great groups have attempted to lower their financial costs, both by supplying more of their financial needs from internal reserves, and by 'shopping around' amongst all the sources of loan finance for cheaper interest rates than they are normally charged when they borrow from group banks. Nevertheless, it is generally agreed that firms belonging to a group can turn to the group bank

Mitsubishi Heavy Industries aircraft manufacturing plant at Nagoya. The MU-2 business plane has been sold all over the world.

or other group financial organs (insurance houses, investment companies, etc) as the last-resort suppliers of loans in times of financial need. The supply of finance from within the group is therefore still probably the strongest single unifying force for each group. There is some evidence that, by charging higher interest rates to other group firms for their loans, the group bank secures for itself a larger proportion of the group's profits than would otherwise be the case. It can use this in various ways to cement its position within the group.

During the last twenty-five years, other powerful ties have developed which justify treating the group as a single entity. The first of these is the existence of close inter-firm contacts at the highest managerial level. The presidents of each of the main companies in the group meet on a regular basis, generally once each month. (Some Japanese observers insist that the group should be defined as consisting of those firms whose presidents attend these famous monthly meetings, although for some purposes the group may be defined as including other firms; for example, the wholly owned subsidiaries of group members.) Though the exact nature of the deliberations at these meetings is not made public, it is generally agreed that matters of high policy which concern the group as a whole are decided in this forum. For example, the decision to go into a new line of industry, or to invest heavily overseas in the exploitation of natural resources, is said to require sanction at this level. In addition, many senior executives sit on the board of more than one firm in the group and there is a frequent exchange of staff at many levels in the administrative and technical hierarchies. It is also common practice for the group bank to despatch high-ranking officers to intervene at managerial level in the affairs of other firms in the group, especially when a firm's performance falls short of expected levels.

Another, very distinctive, way in which firms within a group have established powerful ties with each other is through the exchange of their shares. The pattern that this exchange follows and the extent to which it has occurred is well illustrated in the mutual shareholdings of the twenty-one firms which are represented at the monthly meeting of the Mitsubishi group presidents. Nearly thirty per cent on average of the shares of every firm in the group are owned by other members of the group (the range is from 13·99 per cent for Mitsubishi Oil to 57·39 per cent for Mitsubishi Plastics). Of note too, while the number of shares owned by the manufacturing firms in the group is never negligible and in some cases is quite large, it is the group banks and insurance companies and the general trading company (the Mitsubishi Corporation) who own the most shares in most members of the group. The situation in the five other *keiretsu*, Mitsui, Sumitomo, Fuji (Fuyō), Dai-ichi Kangyō Bank, and Sanwa Bank, is remarkably similar. There are several important implications of this pattern of mutual share ownership. Firstly, the banks and other financial organisations within the groups have acted as the main suppliers of loans to firms within the group. It is very likely that the reason for the gradual acquisition by these institutions of a substantial minority shareholding in the firms to which they have continually loaned money stemmed chiefly from a desire to guarantee themselves a powerful voice in the running of companies in whose affairs they had staked so much. Until 1978, banks could legally own up to ten per cent of the shares of any given company. As a result of an amendment to the 1947 Anti-monopoly Law, made in 1978, the limit was lowered to five per cent.

Secondly, the flow of funds to any firm in the group as the result of the sale of its shares to other group firms could be substantial. In this way, surpluses from accumulated profits could be transferred within the group to any firm with a potentially high rate of return on new investment which needed to be financed.

Thirdly, member firms in a group belong to a wide variety of industries. There is evidence, however, to show that transactions are concentrated, as far as possible, within the group. That is to say, firms tend to buy from, or sell to, other firms within the group rather than do business with firms outside the group. Since all the firms in the group own shares in each other, the cost of orders placed by one firm in that group with another may be partly offset as appreciating share values or as higher dividends – rather like getting trading stamps with your purchases. This kind of benefit is in addition to the economies which may be achieved for the group as a whole through such things as joint advertising. Another example of cost saving available to group firms is the opportunity they have to use the services of the general trading company belonging to the group. These trading companies handle a very large proportion of the group's total sales and purchases, and because of their size, their knowledge of a large number of markets at home and overseas, and the excellence of their information networks, they can handle both a firm's sales and its purchases of raw materials more cheaply than it can itself.

Whilst it is clear that there are considerable benefits for firms in belonging to groups of this kind, the benefits to Japanese society as a whole are rather more questionable. The six *keiretsu* are very large and powerful. Even on the narrowest definitions they control a little under a quarter of all the assets owned by Japanese industry, and account for a similar proportion of its total sales. Rivalry between these groups has produced fierce competition in the many industries in which they come into contact, and the pattern of large-scale new investment has been largely created to defend their relative positions in these various markets. This in turn has been largely responsible for Japan's rapid economic growth. As a result of the economies of scale achieved and the continuous application of the newest technology to the production process, the Japanese consumer has been presented with a wide range of new products at relatively low prices.

However, that does not necessarily mean that the consumer has been presented with the choice of products he has really wanted, or that the prices he has had to pay for them have really reflected the costs of their production. The power of the large groups includes the power to persuade through mass advertising. It also includes the related power to allocate a large proportion of Japan's national resources in a way which may not coincide with the nation's real interests. But, most importantly, these firms are answerable to no-one. The pattern of mutual shareholding amongst firms belonging to these groups means, in effect, that the managers are the shareholders, and the monthly meetings of company presidents of group firms is, in fact, a meeting of the group's major shareholders. Managers are answerable only to other managers.

Government and big business

In this situation, the Government is the only other group with enough power to put pressure on large businesses when they are thought not to be acting in the best interests of the nation as a whole. But big business has very close ties with the ruling Liberal Democratic Party. Not only does the major part of the massive political contributions needed to fight elections come from big business but, in addition, businessmen form a significant proportion of LDP members of the Diet. In the 1970s the feeling grew that the alliance between the Government and big business, whilst it helped to produce the rapid rise in incomes in the 1960s, ought no longer to go unquestioned and unchallenged.

Two sets of events have helped to crystallise this feeling. The first was the public's increasing unease about industrial pollution. This was fed by the publicity given to those extreme cases – like Minamata – which had resulted in death and mutilation on a large scale. Large firms in the chemical and petrochemical industries were very often involved, and their implacable resistance to any attempt to convince them of their responsibility until forced to do so by the Courts both angered the public and reinforced the feeling that big business was really accountable to no-one. The other main influence on the change in public mood was a result of the oil crisis of 1973 and President Nixon's 'shock' measures designed to slow down the rate of penetration of the United States market by Japanese goods. It was eventually discovered that some of the *keiretsu*, usually through their general trading companies, had indulged in large-scale speculation in land, securities, and certain basic commodities such as timber and rice. The oil companies had also formed an illegal cartel to profit from the fears about future oil supplies by under-reporting the size of the stocks and by regulating current supplies. These spectacular discoveries, together with the feeling which had developed over a longer time that prices were being administered by large firms against the interests of consumers, led to the growth of a consumer movement in Japan and to an increasing hostility towards big business.

At the same time, mature reflection in political and academic circles on the nature of Japan's monopoly problem led to proposals for changing the law. The Anti-monopoly Law was finally revised in May 1978. This became possible because the alliance between big business and the ruling party was temporarily weakened, partly as a result of the consumer movement, and partly because Premier Miki, and after him Premier Fukuda, were pledged to cleaner Government. This in turn was the result of the public reaction to Premier Tanaka's corrupt practices in office. It is significant that the law was amended to allow the forcible division of large firms whose monopoly power is thought to exceed acceptable limits, and that it now places stricter upper limits on the proportion of the shares of a firm that can be owned by another firm. This is a direct attack on one of the chief ways by which firms organise themselves into groups, and a recognition that there is at least the possibility that groups may use their power against the best interests of the nation at large.

The new groups: *Kigyō shūdan*

This does not quite conclude what needs to be said about large-scale enterprises in Japan. Most large firms in Japan, including those who belong to *keiretsu*, have large numbers of subsidiaries and affiliated companies. (I use the words 'subsidiary company' to mean one where more than 50 per cent of the shares are owned by a parent company, and 'affiliated company' for a company more than 10 per cent of whose shares are owned by a larger company, which thus may be said to have a controlling interest.) Some of these companies – although they belong to them – are, for all practical purposes, independent of the six great *keiretsu*. They have, moreover, gathered around them such large numbers of subsidiary and affiliated companies of their own that they have come to be considered as the centre of a new kind of group – known in Japanese as *kigyō shūdan*. Some of the biggest of these, like the New Japan Steel Corporation, Matsushita Electric (National Panasonic), Hitachi, Toyota and Nissan have several hundreds of such subsidiary and affiliated companies.

In these *kigyō shūdan*, all the firms in the group are subsidiary or affiliated companies of the large firm at the head of the group, but they do not have any shares in this firm. The top management of the leading firm is therefore able to control the group as a whole. The advantages of group membership belong largely to the leading firm, although group surpluses may be invested in any part of the group. Subsidiary firms are often small, so that by sub-contracting work to these firms the leading firm can take advantage of the lower labour costs of small firms. Generally speaking, firms in these groups are also vertically integrated – that is to say the whole production process, from the first operations on the raw materials to the final sale of the products, whether they are television sets or motor cars, are undertaken within the group; and this also tends to reduce costs significantly. In the same way, vertical integration makes it easier for such firms to maximise their profits by operating close controls over the supply of their products. The number of distributors is limited and they are owned by the leading firm. The prices of the products and the rate at which they are allowed to come on to the market are therefore under group control and can be manipulated to the advantage of the group. Once again the actions of the group are only modified as a result of the reactions of other equally powerful groups, while collusion between groups – though notoriously difficult to prove – is frequently suspected. Competition is not between firm and firm but between group and group, and its true nature can only be completely understood when the relationship between groups is understood. The recent amendments to the Anti-monopoly Law, particularly the upper limits on the value of the shares a firm can own, will at least restrain the tendency of these groups to become even larger, although their present strength has not been affected.

The dynamics of competition in Japanese industry have therefore been largely unaffected by the crises of the early 1970s, and they will continue to provide Japan with an economic growth-rate higher than most other industrial countries. The worst excesses in the behaviour of large firms have certainly been somewhat modified. The new anti-monopoly legislation also marks an attempt to redress the imbalance of economic power in Japanese society. Nevertheless, the most interesting changes in Japan's economic structure in the 1970s have not occurred in Japanese industry.

The changing role of Government

Until the start of the 1970s, the Japanese government played only a minor role in Japan's economic life, since its annual expenditure – at least in comparison with the industrial nations of the West – was extremely low. For example, government expenditure as a proportion of the gross national product was slightly under seventeen per cent in Japan in 1970, whilst the equivalent figure, averaged for the United Kingdom, the United States, France, Germany, and Italy for the period 1970 to 1972, was nearly thirty-three per cent. As tax revenues rose with growing incomes, successive Governments have therefore been able not just to finance such expenditure as they wished, but also to balance their budgets and even produce a surplus.

The breakdown of government expenditure also reveals significant differences between Japan and other industrial countries. Firstly, military expenditure has been very small when compared with North America and Western Europe. Secondly, until the mid-1970s, relatively little was spent on social welfare. Where the Government did spend heavily was for investment in transport facilities, sites for industry, etc, which would enhance the profitability of private industry and help sustain its high rate of growth.

In the early years of the 1970s, there were increasing doubts about the desirability of allowing existing economic policies to continue unchallenged. 'Economic growth for whom?' was the question that came to be asked, and this was stimulated by the worsening of industrial pollution and by the realisation that the quality of life for large sectors of the population (especially the elderly) was not being improved even by economic growth of the rapidity achieved in Japan. In this climate of opinion the Government's reluctance to play a more active role came to be more frequently questioned. On the problem of social welfare, for example, an International Labour Organization report showed that in 1971 total Government expenditure in Japan on social security was only 5·7 per cent of her gross domestic product. The equivalent figure for the United States was 10·5 per cent, for the United Kingdom 14 per cent, for West Germany 17·3 per cent, and for countries like Sweden and Holland over 20 per cent. It is true that company-based welfare and retirement pension schemes dating from before the Second World War had, in many cases, been modernised in the 1960s; but these were confined to relatively few firms employing only a small proportion of the total number of workers. The existence of these schemes, combined with the fact that almost all the Government's social security payments were so low, resulted in sharp differences between the employed and the unemployed, and between those working in large and those working in small firms. These official payments were also heavily concentrated on assistance with medical expenses in times of illness, with a startling neglect of areas like pensions. At the beginning of the 1970s, therefore, the Government's social security system was not only underdeveloped but heavily biased towards provision during people's working life, when economic risk is relatively low, with poor provision for people's nonworking life when this risk is much higher.

The undesirability of this state of affairs was impressed on the Government in the 1970s by social scientists, who pointed out that social and demographic trends in Japan meant that changes in the Government's attitude were urgent and imperative, particularly in the case of the elderly. In common with all industrial countries Japan's population is ageing, but it is ageing unusually fast. The proportion of those over sixty-five to those of working age was 8·9 per cent in 1960. In 1975 it was 11·6 per cent, in 1980 over thirteen per cent and by the end of the century it will be around twenty-one per cent. Whereas until recently the extended family has been the norm in Japanese society, this has now been replaced by the nuclear family of three or four persons. This means that family support for the elderly is less forthcoming and will have to be replaced or supplemented by state support.

In the last few years the Government has begun to respond to the need for greater expenditure on social welfare. In the first place a larger share of the nation's total resources has been devoted to social security payments. These have increased from 1,866,968 million yen (6·1 per cent of the national income) in 1966 to 14,579,639 million yen (10·6 per cent of national income) in 1976. The proportions of the various categories of welfare payments have also been altered. There has for example been a serious attempt to meet the demands imposed by an ageing population, since pensions have increased from 224,406 million yen (10·6 per cent of the total) to 4,073,949 million yen (27·9 per cent of the total) in 1976. Nevertheless, with little more than ten per cent of her national income going into welfare payments of all kinds in 1980, Japan is still considerably behind other advanced industrial nations. The problem of the aged, in particular, is a long way from being solved.

Government expenditure in Japan is still much smaller than in many other countries in North America and Western Europe. Measured in constant (1970) prices the proportion of such public spending in gross national expenditure was 16·8 per cent in 1970, rose to 18·4 per cent in 1975 but had fallen back to 16·2 per cent in 1977. Besides some redirection of this spending during the 1970s to meet more pressing social problems, the Government has also taken a greater interest in the provision of goods and services which private industry was little inclined to produce, such as housing for the less well-off sections of the population. However, a commitment to raise public expenditure substantially would be a clear break with tradition. It would require either a substantial increase in taxation, at a time when Japan is being urged to maintain her rate of economic growth in order to prevent a further decline in the international economy; or it would entail a change in the level of the Government's debt and in the system of financing it. This too would have far-reaching consequences for the way in which the Government has controlled the level of economic activity and for its traditional policy of encouraging economic growth. The Government has been very cautious about doing anything, including responding to pressing social needs, which would speed up this change beyond what it calculates is an acceptable rate. It is difficult to escape the conclusion, indeed, that no Japanese Government is yet prepared to face up to the problem.

Conclusion

The future of the Japanese economy is uncertain. The important position which Japan has carved out for herself in the world economy depends, more than anything else, on a large and readily available supply of imported raw materials – especially oil. If nationalism strengthens in the countries which supply these raw materials, or if there is a radical change in attitude towards the rate at which such non-renewable resources ought to be exploited, then it is difficult to see how Japan can continue to achieve the competitive advantage she has maintained in many world markets over the last twenty years. At the very least she will have to learn to cope with the problems of slower economic growth and – which might be even more significant in the longer term – with growing claims for a fairer distribution of the wealth which she already produces.

5
Politics and politicians

Graham Healey

Introduction

Japan has had a constitutional system of government, with a wholly or
partly elected parliament (the Diet), for nearly a hundred years. That is
not to say, of course, that Japan has been for the last century what we
would now recognise as a parliamentary democracy – few countries
have. But it is important to understand that the Japanese experience of
a parliamentary system, and of the political parties and elections that go
with it, extends unbroken over several generations. The constitution has
never been suspended and elections have never been discontinued; no
period longer than five years has passed without a general election since
1890, and the average interval between elections has been less than three
years. Political parties have often been harassed and at times suppressed,
and all the leading parties performed an act of self-immolation when
they joined the Imperial Rule Assistance Association in 1940, but party
activity has never entirely ceased since its beginnings in the 1870s, even
during the 'fascist' 1930s. The parties that were formed immediately
after the Second World War were, for the most part, the pre-war parties
under new names, with the same leaders and similar programmes.
Before 1945, other groups (the former *samurai*, the bureaucracy, the
army and navy) usually wielded greater power and could overbear or
manipulate the Diet, which consequently, for most of the period from
the establishment of the parliamentary system in 1890 to the surrender
of August 1945, played a minor role in Japanese politics. But the 'democratisation' process carried out under the Occupation was far from
being a complete break with the past: Japan's pre-war experience of
parliamentary institutions has had a considerable influence on the character of contemporary politics.

The new Constitution and the new Diet (1945 – 1947)

Unlike Germany's, Japan's system of government did not collapse in 1945. The Occupation authorities (SCAP) ruled indirectly, through the Emperor and the Diet: SCAP issued 'administrative directives', which were translated either into Imperial Ordinances or into legislation.

There had been no proposals in the pre-surrender planning for any revision of the Japanese Constitution, which was not thought to be an insuperable obstacle to the creation of a genuinely democratic system of government. Shidehara Kijūrō, Prime Minister from October 1945 to May 1946, believed that it would not be necessary to revise the constitution, merely to put an end to abuses in its application; and it is true that some radical legislation (on land reform and female suffrage, for example) was enacted in 1946 and early 1947 while the old constitution was still in force. Most of the earliest reforms, however, were carried out not through the Diet but through Imperial Ordinances which, the Occupation authorities feared, could be rescinded with little difficulty once the Occupation had ended. SCAP was certainly convinced by October 1945 of the need to give greater permanency to the Occupation reforms by amending the constitution.

Lawyers in the SCAP Government Section drafted a model for the consideration of the Japanese Government, and the Constitution that eventually came into force in May 1947, having passed through the Diet and the Privy Council in the guise of a 'revision' of the Constitution of 1889, bears the stamp of their New Deal liberalism. The preamble proclaims that 'sovereign power resides in the people' and that 'government is a sacred trust of the people, the authority for which is derived from the people, the powers of which are exercised by the representatives of the people, and the benefits of which are enjoyed by the people'. The Emperor is merely 'the symbol of the State and of the unity of the people, deriving his position from the will of the people'. Chapter III guarantees 'the fundamental human rights' (including the right to 'life, liberty and the pursuit of happiness'), equality under the law, freedom of thought, of conscience, of religion, of assembly and association, of speech, of the press, and of 'all other forms of expression'.

The National Diet, under this Constitution, is 'the highest organ of state power . . . the sole law-making organ of the state'. It comprises an upper chamber, the House of Councillors, and a lower chamber, the House of Representatives, both of which 'shall consist of elected members, representative of all the people'. The term of office of members of the House of Representatives is four years, but the House may be dissolved before that term is up, in which case a general election must be held within forty days. Members of the House of Councillors serve a six-year term, half of the seats being contested every three years. The House

The National Diet building in Tokyo, seat of both houses of the Japanese legislature.

of Councillors cannot be dissolved; it is normally closed whenever the House of Representatives is dissolved, but if necessary it may be convoked in emergency session by the Cabinet.

The House of Representatives is the more powerful. A bill must normally be passed by both Houses to become law, but one passed by the House of Representatives and rejected by the House of Councillors becomes law if passed a second time by a two-thirds' majority of the House of Representatives. The budget must be submitted first to the House of Representatives. If the House of Councillors fails to agree to a budget (or to a treaty) that has been passed by the House of Representatives, the decision of the House of Representatives becomes, after a prescribed period, the decision of the Diet.

Executive power is vested in the Cabinet, which is collectively responsible to the Diet. The Prime Minister is designated by the Diet from among its own number. He and the Ministers of State he appoints, a majority of whom are to be chosen from among the members of the Diet, must all be civilians. The House of Representatives can force the resignation of the Cabinet, or its own dissolution, by passing a vote of no confidence (as it did, to its own astonishment, in May 1980).

The Diet's powers, however, are not unlimited. The whole judicial power is vested in the courts, and the court of last resort, the Supreme Court, has the power 'to determine the constitutionality of any law, order, regulation or official act'.

The Electoral System

The franchise was extended to all citizens over the age of twenty by a revision of the House of Representatives Election Law carried out in December 1945, well before the promulgation of the new Constitution.

The Constitution's promise that 'the people have the inalienable right to choose their public officials and to dismiss them' is embodied in the Public Offices Election Law of 1950 which, as well as determining the eligibility of citizens to vote and to stand for office, prescribes the method of voting and the constituency system. Under this law each of 130 constituencies returns (with a few exceptions) from three to five members to the 511-seat House of Representatives. Each elector may vote for one candidate only; the vote is not transferable. The three, four, or five candidates (depending on the size of the constituency) who receive most votes are elected. The system of election for the House of Councillors is rather more complex: 152 members are elected from the prefectures (the forty-five local government units into which Japan is divided) and 100 from the 'national constituency' – that is, the country as a whole.

Every electoral system puts some parties at an advantage and others at a disadvantage. The system of election by a relative majority in single-member constituencies – the 'first-past-the-post' system used in British parliamentary elections – results in over-representation of the large parties and under-representation of the small ones. (At the British general election of May 1979, for example, the Conservative Party, with 43·9 per cent of votes, won 53·3 per cent of seats, and the Labour Party, with 36·9 per cent of votes, won 42·2 per cent of seats. The Liberal Party however, in spite of polling 13·8 per cent of votes, won only 1·7 per cent of seats). The merit claimed for this system is that it creates stability by ensuring single-party majorities in parliament. The system of proportional representation (PR), although it comes closest to reflecting in the distribution of seats the actual support among the electorate for each party, is said by supporters of the 'first-past-the-post' system to result in

Above
Election posters.
Candidates for
Tokyo's municipal
elections in
April 1979.

Below
Victory celebration.
In his excitement,
the successful
candidate has
painted in the left
eye of the Daruma
(the traditional
good luck symbol)
with rather less
finesse than when
he painted in
the right eye
at the beginning
of the campaign.

A demonstration by students at Kyōto University. In the late 1960's Japanese students were among the most militant in the world. Now only a committed minority of radicals survive.

the fragmentation of parties and the formation of unstable coalition governments.

The 'semi-proportional' Japanese system lies somewhere between the two, and might reasonably claim the virtues of both. Admittedly, the parties with the largest shares of the popular vote usually win disproportionately large shares of seats: the Liberal Democratic Party won between 5·8 per cent and 11·7 per cent more seats than votes at every election between 1960 and 1980, and the Japan Socialist Party had a similar 'bonus' of 2–3 per cent at most elections during this period. The smaller parties conversely win fewer seats than they would under the PR system: the Japan Communist Party, for example, won 9·8 per cent of votes in 1980, but only 5·7 per cent of seats. But the discrepancy is less than under the British system – less indeed than under any other non-PR system. At the same time the system produced a single-party majority at ten of the thirteen elections between 1947 and 1980.

One other important feature of Japanese elections is the disparity in the size of constituencies; the rural areas are over-represented and the urban areas under-represented. In the 1980 House of Representatives election, the most under-represented constituency, Chiba No 4, had 323,184 voters per seat, while the most over-represented, Hyōgo No 5, had only 81,695. In other words, one vote in Hyōgo was worth nearly four votes in Chiba. Some candidates in densely-populated urban constituencies therefore fail to win seats even though they receive several times as many votes as some successful candidates in rural constituencies. In the 1980 election, for example, an LDP candidate in Kagawa was elected with only 35,435 votes, whereas a Communist candidate in Hokkaidō who received 125,714 votes failed to win a seat. There are many similar examples of this phenomenon.

The reason for this imbalance is that both the constituency boundaries, and the number of members to be returned by each constituency, were fixed immediately after the Second World War, when the rural population was much greater in relation to the urban population than it is now. This imbalance benefits the ruling Liberal Democratic Party (the LDP), whose principal support lies in the rural areas, and it has been a major factor in maintaining a conservative majority in the Diet. If the constituencies were all of exactly the same size we should expect that in any House of Representatives election the 511 candidates who received most votes would be elected, or at least that the number of successful candidates who came below 511th place in a list of all candidates ranked in order of votes won would be very small. But of the members of the House of Representatives elected in 1976, for example, seventy-four fell below 511th place. Of these, forty-one were LDP members. After the House of Representatives election of 1972, voters in Chiba No 1 constituency tried to have the results of the election declared invalid on the grounds that the inequality in the size of constituencies violated Article 14 of the Constitution, which guarantees equality under the law. In April 1976, the Supreme Court declared that the unequal size of constituencies was indeed a breach of the Constitution, but decided that it would not be in the public interest to strike down the election results. A similar attempt was made to challenge the results of the 1976 election, but by the time the case reached the Supreme Court in December 1979 the House of Representatives elected in 1976 had been dissolved and a new election held. The Supreme Court consequently refused to give judgment.

Attempts have been made from time to time to reduce the anomalies in constituency size by giving more Diet seats to the most under-represented urban constituencies (the number of seats in the House of Representatives has risen from 466 in 1945 to 511 now), but the Diet cannot continue indefinitely to increase in size; and a real *redistribution* of seats, which would mean reducing the representation of some rural constituencies, would be extremely difficult politically for the LDP. The LDP indeed has long favoured the adoption of the 'first-past-the-post' system, which would greatly increase its electoral advantage, but the proposal has met with implacable opposition from the other parties.

Political Parties

Immediately after Japan's surrender in 1945 the two major pre-war parties were re-established under new names: the Liberal Party, descended from one wing of the Seiyūkai, founded in 1900 and the successor of the Patriotic Society, Japan's first political party; and the Progressive Party, composed of several groups of the old Minseitō founded in 1927, but also the successor of an earlier party, Rikken Dōshikai, founded in 1913. In the first post-war general election, in April 1946, these two conservative parties won slightly over half the seats in the House of Representatives, and the Japan Socialist Party, formed from the pre-war 'proletarian' parties, nearly a quarter.

Most established politicians had been purged from public life by the Occupation authorities in the early part of 1946. Consequently, most of those who won seats at this election were newcomers to the Diet. Yoshida Shigeru, a former Foreign Office man who had no parliamentary experience and no previous connection with any party, became leader of the Liberal Party in 1946 and served as Prime Minister for almost the whole of the period 1946 to 1954. There formed around him within the Liberal Party a 'Yoshida faction' comprising, as well as those few party men who had escaped purging, a number of newly-elected former bureaucrats (such as Ikeda Hayato and Satō Eisaku, who between them were to hold the office of Prime Minister through the whole of the 1960s). After 1951

'depurged' conservative politicians began to return to politics. They formed an intra-party 'opposition' to the Yoshida men, who were by now well-established and experienced parliamentarians. After several years of strife, Yoshida lost the Prime-Ministership to Hatoyama Ichirō, the leader of this 'opposition', in December 1954.

The Progressive Party was similarly divided; it was fundamentally a conservative party, but contained a reformist as well as a traditionalist wing. After the 1947 election the Progressives, together with the small Co-operative Party, entered into a coalition government led by the Socialist Party, which had won the largest number of seats. Less than a year later the Socialist Party leader, Katayama Tetsu, was replaced as Prime Minister by the Progressives' leader, Ashida Hitoshi. Within another nine months the coalition collapsed and the majority of Progressives threw in their lot with the Liberals, who at the next election, in 1949, won an overall majority in the House of Representatives.

During this first post-war decade, the left was no more united than the right. The Japan Socialist Party was successor to a number of small pre-war parties of varying ideological hues. As a result, it was composed of a right wing associated with 'moderate' labour unions, a Marxist left wing, and a centre group, which was weakened by the purging of many of its members. In the first few years after the surrender the JSP was dominated by its right wing, but after the failure of the coalition of 1947

163

and 1948 the party's centre of gravity shifted towards the left. In 1951 the party split over the peace treaty issue. The left wing would countenance only a 'total' peace settlement that included the Soviet Union, but the right wing was prepared to support the San Francisco Treaty, to which the Soviet Union was not a party.

The 1949 election had been a debacle for the JSP – it won only forty-eight seats – but during the early 1950s, largely as a result of Japan's economic hardships, electoral support for the socialists increased rapidly, in spite of the split in the party. In 1952 the left and right-wing socialists together won 111 seats; in 1953 they won 138; and in 1955 they won 156. The combined representation of the conservative parties, meanwhile, fell from 333 to 297. Seeing the possibility of taking power, the left and right wing socialists came together again in October 1955. The conservatives were greatly alarmed by the threat from the re-united Japan Socialist Party (the JSP), and within a few weeks the Liberal Party and the Progressives (which had been renamed the Democratic Party in October 1952) themselves came together to form the Liberal Democratic Party (the LDP).

Thus in the autumn of 1955 a balance of a kind was struck between the two major parliamentary groups, conservatives and 'progressives'. A two-party system seemed to be developing. At the next three elections (those of 1958, 1960 and 1963) the LDP and JSP between them won well over eighty per cent of the popular vote and well over ninety per cent of Diet seats. The ratio between the two parties however was consistently two-to-one in favour of the LDP. What had in fact arisen was a 'one-and-a-half' party system. The LDP and JSP have had comparable shares of the vote in urban areas, but the LDP has had a much larger share of the rural vote and has thus been able to stay permanently in office. In this it has been aided by the fact that the rural constituencies are over-represented, so that, even when its share of the popular vote has fallen below fifty per cent, it has continued to have a majority in the Diet. This majority was reduced to a bare minimum in the late 1970s, but the 1980 election gave back to the LDP the kind of dominating position in both Houses of the Diet that it had held in the 1960s.

The *Liberal Democratic Party* (LDP), which has now ruled Japan for a quarter of a century, is essentially the party of big business and the bureaucracy. Conservative politicians may be divided into 'party men' who have served long political apprenticeships, often as members of town, city, or prefectural assemblies, and 'bureaucrats' who have stepped sideways into politics after careers in government service. It is the bureaucrats who have dominated conservative politics since the war: eight of the thirteen post-war Prime Ministers have been former government officials. This close connection between the ruling party and the bureaucracy has had its effect on the character of government. Most legislation is instigated by one or other of the ministries, and first examined in the Diet by one of the standing committees, whose research staffs are headed by ministry officials, and whose chairmen are often themselves former bureaucrats, ready to see the ministry's point of view. The LDP also has close connections with big business, from which it derives most of its funds. Many conservative politicians have business backgrounds.

In fact, the relationship among the LDP leadership, the bureaucracy and the business world is a triangular one. Many of those senior bureaucrats who do not enter politics on retirement from the Civil Service go into industry and commerce. An official of the Ministry of Construction, for example, may join a big construction firm, where he will be able to put to good use his knowledge of the workings of the ministry and his personal relationships both with colleagues still serving and with those who have gone into politics.

Between 1960 and 1976, the proportion of the popular vote won by the LDP fell steadily. (It rose somewhat at the elections of 1979 and 1980, but remained below fifty per cent.) The decline in popularity of the LDP was not, however, accompanied by an increase in support for the Japan Socialist Party (the JSP); it too has had a falling share of the vote in urban areas. In cities such as Tokyo and Ōsaka it is now often third, fourth or even last among the opposition parties.

The *Japan Socialist Party* (JSP) relies for most of its support on Sōhyō, the largest and most radical of the labour union federations. A high proportion of the party's candidates in elections are trades unionists, who make use of their union's, rather than the party's, organisation and funds for campaign purposes. This dependence on Sōhyō, and the departure of the party's right wing in a final split in 1960, has given the JSP a narrowly left-wing base, and its electoral appeal has declined steadily.

Between 1960 and 1980, the proportion of the popular vote won by the LDP and the JSP together fell from 85·12 per cent to 67·21 per cent, a decline of nearly a quarter (see Table 1). Where have the votes gone?

In the 1950s the only other substantial party in existence was the *Japan Communist Party* (JCP). Its support was then very limited, but during the 1960s its popularity increased considerably. In the seventies it announced that it would follow a line independent of both the Soviet and Chinese parties, and also began to cultivate grass-roots support through the provision of free medical treatment, legal advice, and other practical help, rather than through propaganda. Ever since 1972 the JCP's share of the popular vote has remained steady at about ten per cent. The number of seats the party has been able to win with this proportion of the vote however has fluctuated considerably (see Table 2).

Since 1960 four new parties have been established: the Democratic Socialist Party (DSP); the Kōmeitō, or Clean Government Party; the New

Table 1 : Distribution of the popular vote at General Elections, 1960 to 1980

	1960	1963	1967	1969	1972	1976	1979	1980
LDP	22,740,271	22,423,915	22,447,838	22,381,570	24,563,199	23,655,624	24,084,127	28,262,438
	57·76%	54·67%	48·80%	47·63%	46·85%	41·78%	44·59%	47·90%
JSP	10,887,134	11,906,766	12,826,103	10,074,100	11,478,742	11,713,005	10,643,448	11,400,742
	27·56%	29·03%	27·89%	21·44%	21·90%	20·69%	19·71%	19·31%
DSP	3,464,147	3,023,302	3,404,463	3,636,590	3,660,953	3,554,075	3,663,691	3,896,728
	8·77%	7·37%	7·40%	7·74%	6·98%	6·27%	6·78%	6·60%
JCP	1,156,723	1,646,477	2,190,563	3,199,031	5,496,827	5,878,192	5,625,526	5,803,612
	2·93%	4·01%	4·76%	6·81%	10·49%	10·38%	10·42%	9·83%
Kōmeitō*	—	—	2,472,371	5,124,666	4,436,755	6,177,300	5,282,682	5,329,941
			5·38%	10·91%	8·46%	10·91%	9·78%	9·03%
Minor Parties	141,941	59,765	101,244	81,373	143,019	45,113	69,100	109,167
	0·35%	0·15%	0·22%	0·17%	0·27%	0·08%	0·13%	0·18%
Independents†	1,118,905	1,956,313	2,553,998	2,492,560	2,645,582	3,227,462	2,641,063	2,056,966
	2·83%	4·77%	5·55%	5·30%	5·05%	5·70%	4·88%	3·48%
NLC*	—	—	—	—	—	2,363,984	1,631,811	1,766,396
						4·18%	3·02%	2·99%
USD*	—	—	—	—	—	—	368,660	402,832
							0·68%	0·68%
Totals	39,509,121	41,016,538	45,996,570	46,989,890	52,425,077	56,614,755	54,010,108	59,028,822

Liberal Club (NLC); and the United Social Democratic Party (USD). The votes and seats won by these parties (in 1980, a total of over 11,000,000 votes and eighty seats) would in earlier days have gone for the most part to the LDP and JSP, although there is reason to believe that the Kōmeitō has won many of its seats at the expense of the Japan Communist Party by competing with it for the votes of the urban poor.

The *Democratic Socialist Party* (DSP) was founded in January 1960 when the right wing of the JSP, including fifty-nine Diet members, broke away from the party. Its leaders were pragmatists who set their faces against what they regarded as the doctrinaire 'oppositionism' of the JSP and JCP. The party has often allied itself with the LDP, particularly in local government elections, and has also worked hard to establish an anti-communist coalition of 'middle-of-the-road progressive' parties. The DSP is supported by Dōmei, the All-Japan Federation of Labour. Dōmei, the second of the two major labour federations, is based on the unions of private industry. Its members do not however seem to follow their leaders in their choice of party; the DSP has little support from the mass of industrial workers. It lagged well behind both the JCP and the Kōmeitō

---

* The Kōmeitō first put up candidates for the House of Representatives in 1967; the New Liberal Club first did so in 1976; and the United Social Democratic Party in 1979.
† Most of the successful 'independent' candidates joined the LPD on entering the Diet.

Table 2: Distribution of seats in the House of Representatives at General Elections, 1960 to 1980

	1960	1963	1967	1969	1972	1976	1979	1980
LDP	296	283	277	288	271	249	248	284
	63·4%	60·6%	57·0%	59·3%	55·2%	48·7%	48·5%	55·6%
JSP	145	144	140	90	118	123	107	107
	31·0%	30·8%	28·8%	18·5%	24·0%	24·1%	20·9%	20·9%
DSP	17	23	30	31	19	29	35	32
	3·6%	4·9%	6·2%	6·4%	3·9%	5·6%	6·8%	6·3%
JCP	3	5	5	14	38	17	39	29
	0·6%	1·1%	1·0%	2·9%	7·7%	3·3%	7·6%	5·7%
Kōmeitō	—	—	25	47	29	55	57	33
			5·1%	9·7%	5·9%	10·8%	11·2%	6·5%
Minor Parties	1	0	0	0	2	0	0	0
	0·2%				0·4%			
Independents	5	12	9	16	14	21	19	11
	1·1%	2·6%	1·9%	3·3%	2·9%	4·1%	3·7%	2·1%
NLC	—	—	—	—	—	17	4	12
						3·3%	0·8%	2·3%
USD	—	—	—	—	—	—	2	3
							0·4%	0·6%
Totals	467	467	486	486	491	511	511	511

in the proportion of the popular vote that it won in 1980, although it was more successful than either in turning votes into seats.

The *Kōmeitō* was founded in 1964 as the political arm of the Sōka Gakkai, or Value Creation Society, an aggressively proselytising sect of Nichiren Buddhism which claims to have over 16,000,000 adherents. The Sōka Gakkai offers material and physical salvation in this world: only believe and pray, and you will enter a new life. Members relate how this man, who before his conversion was a work-shy drunk whose wife and children went in fear of him, is now sober, kind, hard-working, and prosperous, or how that woman's stomach cancer was cured overnight through the power of prayer. Its appeal has been to the economically insecure of the big cities, those of the lower and lower-middle classes who were untouched by the vaunted economic miracle, except to find that it had sent up the prices of their food and clothing and polluted their environment.

The Kōmeitō formally separated itself from the Sōka Gakkai in 1970. There had been much unfavourable publicity about the methods of 'conversion' used by the Sōka Gakkai, and it was feared that this would harm the Kōmeitō electorally. The party tried to broaden its membership to include people who were not adherents of the parent organisation, but with very little success; all its officers and the vast majority of its members still belong to the Sōka Gakkai, whose intricate national organisation is the foundation of the Kōmeitō's election campaigning.

The *New Liberal Club* (NLC) was formed in June 1976 by six young LDP Diet members who left the party in disgust at attempts to cover up the Lockheed scandal. (A number of politicians, businessmen, and officials had been accused of soliciting, accepting or transmitting bribes from the Lockheed aircraft corporation, which had been trying to secure Japanese orders for Lockheed planes.) In terms of policy, the NLC is virtually indistinguishable from the LDP, which it has consistently supported in important Diet votes. What it seeks to represent is a conservatism uncorrupted by too-close links with big business. In the summer of 1979, the NLC split over the issue of whether it was to be in truth a new conservative party or merely a ginger-group whose only aim was to improve the tone of the LDP. In the election of that October the party did very badly, although its fortunes improved in the 1980 election.

The *United Social Democratic Party* (USD) was formally constituted in March 1978 by a number of right-wing JSP members who had broken away from the party during the course of the previous year. It has so far won little support.

Party support and voting behaviour

The votes cast at Japanese elections are commonly categorised as 'conservative' (those cast for the LDP and conservative independents), 'progressive' (those cast for the JSP, the JCP and 'progressive' independents), and 'middle-of-the-road' (those cast for the Kōmeito, the DSP, the NLC and the USD). It cannot be assumed, however, that every elector who casts his vote for one of the candidates of a particular party at a given election is a committed 'ideological' supporter of the party. During the 1970s an increasing proportion of the electorate said, in public opinion polls, that they were not committed to any party; an *Asahi Shinbun* poll taken less than two weeks before the 1980 election found that over thirty-five per cent of voters fell into this category. These uncommitted voters are not evenly distributed, either geographically or demographically; they are more numerous in the cities, more often young than old, more often male than female, and more often white-collar workers or labourers than farmers or skilled factory hands. They are, in other words, people in whom the sense of solidarity to be found in, say, the village or the labour union is likely to be weakest. A large proportion declare themselves uncommitted on principle rather than simply 'don't knows'. It follows, of course, that the number of voters who say they *are* committed to one party or another has become progressively smaller. Just before the general election of 1963, for example, forty-six per cent of respondents in a *Mainichi Shinbun* poll said they supported the LDP and twenty-seven per cent that they supported the JSP. In a *Yomiuri Shinbun* poll taken at the time of the 1979 election, thirty-nine per cent claimed to support the LDP and only fourteen per cent the JSP.

In Japan, as in other countries, there is a strong correlation between party support and such variables as age, occupation and level of education. (It is perhaps worth mentioning that religion is of no significance in this connection.) Support for the LDP increases steadily with the age of the voter; it is lowest among voters in their twenties and highest among those over sixty. Support for the JSP and the DSP is low among the youngest voters and lower still among the oldest; it reaches a peak among voters in their forties. In the 1960s support for both these parties was highest among those in their twenties and early thirties; their support in other words has become 'middle-aged' over the last decade. The JCP has a relatively high proportion of young supporters, although it has recently lost ground among those in their twenties. Support for the two newest parties, the NLC and the USD, is highest among the young and declines sharply with age. This is perhaps unsurprising, as both parties came into existence in protest against the entrenched leadership of established parties. (In absolute terms, of course, their support is very small.) Support for the Kōmeitō, interestingly, is above average among the youngest voters, but is otherwise spread evenly over the whole age range.

There is a marked correlation between age and level of education among LDP supporters. Fewer than twenty per cent of university graduates in their twenties support the LDP, but the proportion rises very steeply with increasing age; nearly seventy per cent of university graduates in their late fifties are LDP supporters. There is a similar rise among those with a high-school education, but support for the LDP among those with only an elementary school education falls steadily after the age of thirty, rising again slightly after the age of fifty. This chimes with the fact that the largest single category among supporters of the JSP is that of elementary school graduates in their thirties. The JCP also has a high level of support from this group, but its highest levels of support are among university, high-school and middle-school graduates in their late twenties and early thirties. The Kōmeitō appears to have virtually no support among university graduates over forty.

By occupation, the LDP commands the support of over half of those engaged in agriculture, forestry and fishing, and over forty per cent of managers and self-employed people. The JSP's support is highest among white-collar and blue-collar workers, but even in these two categories it does not achieve higher levels of support than the LDP. It is interesting to note, by the way, that support for the LDP rises with age among white-collar workers but not among blue-collar workers. This is probably attributable to the fact that the white-collar worker receives steady promotion as he gets older. The highest level of support for the Kōmeitō is among workers in small enterprises such as shops. Those who fall under the poll-takers' heading of 'others and unemployed' are also more likely to support the Kōmeitō than any other party. The JCP and DSP both find their highest levels of support among white-collar and industrial workers, whilst the supporters of the NLC and USD are most likely to be white-collar workers or managers, although a fair proportion of the NLC's supporters are the employees of small enterprises. Every party except the LDP and NLC has its lowest level of support among people working in agriculture, forestry, and fishing.

One significant feature of Japanese electoral behaviour is the strong contrast in Japan between town and country; urban and rural voters display some marked differences in attitudes. In rural areas there is much less mobility of residence than in the towns and a stronger sense of community or locality. Country people, therefore, tend to show a greater interest in local politics than city-dwellers do. In rural areas political information and opinion is also more commonly passed on through informal conversation with relatives and neighbours. Personal knowledge of candidates, or of others prominently involved in the political process, looms large in the voter's perception of politics. In the cities, this is true to some extent at the level of the local assembly, but in general the character of the urban community encourages greater interest in national rather than local politics.

Turnout is normally high in Japan, both at national and local elections. At the 1980 general election, 74·5 per cent of the electorate voted; the 1979 turnout of 68 per cent was exceptionally low. Rural voters, apparently because their stronger sense of community leads them to see voting as a social obligation, record higher rates of turnout than urban voters: in 1980, the highest voting rate (87·61 per cent) was achieved in the predominantly rural Shimane Prefecture, and the lowest turnouts were in the big cities of Osaka (67·40 per cent), Tokyo (67·49 per cent) and Kyōto (67·89 per cent). In rural areas, even higher turnouts are recorded at local elections. This is probably because the voter is often acquainted with, or has personal knowledge of, the candidates, and has a stronger sense of his ability to influence politics at this level.

At an election at village level the inhabitants of each of the (perhaps fairly widely-scattered) hamlets that make up the 'village' as a local government unit will often vote *en bloc* to secure the election of their candidate. In a village where one hamlet is dominant because of its size, the inhabitants of the other hamlets may join together, taking it in turns to provide an agreed candidate and using their combined votes to defeat the candidate of the dominant hamlet. Solidarity at this level is such that it is (or used to be) common for communities to set a watch on the roads to look out for campaigners on behalf of candidates from elsewhere. These rival campaigners, if they were bold enough to enter the hamlet,

The opening of the
municipal election
campaign in
Yokosuka, April 1979.

Above
One candidate
displays the
traditional Daruma
to an appreciative
crowd and –
below
another one paints
in the right eye of
his Daruma under
the eaves of the
local shrine.

would be unnerved by being followed silently everywhere they went, or might even be forcibly ejected.

   Political parties are in many respects less important as determinants of voting behaviour in Japan than in, for example, Britain, where it is generally accepted that the personal qualities of the candidates usually make relatively little difference to the outcome of an election. All the British voter needs to know about the candidates is which parties they represent; he votes, it appears, for a particular Government rather than for a representative of his locality, and therefore chooses among parties, each representing a range of policies, rather than among individual candidates with particular qualifications to represent him or his locality. A large proportion of Japanese voters, however, say that it is the quality of the *candidate*, rather than his party affiliation, that determines which way they cast their votes. This is especially true in local elections. Candidates often have no formal party affiliation in elections at the

Campaign workers putting up election posters in the streets.

village or town level, although party endorsement does become more important at higher levels. His standing in the community from which he looks for his support is therefore of particular importance to the Japanese politician.

Getting elected

All that Japanese election law requires of a candidate is that he should declare his candidacy in writing to the appropriate returning officer and pay his deposit. For various reasons, however, few candidates take quite such a straight-forward course.

For one thing, self-effacement is the norm in Japanese society; to let it appear that you *want* public office is to seem objectionably concerned with your own interest as opposed to that of the community. It is much better to be requested to stand. This is especially true in rural areas. The aspiring candidate will allow it to be known that he would be willing to stand for election if it were thought that he would thereby be serving the community. A candidate will often be nominated unanimously by a hamlet of perhaps several dozen households. For local elections it is not usually thought necessary to seek the endorsement of a political party, but for elections at the prefectural and national level, party endorsement does became necessary. Such endorsement is however not always easy to secure. The nature of the constituency system is such that parties must consider their endorsement tactics with great care. Take, for example, a constituency returning three members in which the likely distribution of the vote is: LDP thirty-five per cent, JSP twenty-five per cent, Kōmeitō twenty per cent, DSP twenty per cent. If the LDP puts up only one candidate it will win one seat; but if it puts up two candidates, and the party's supporters divide evenly between them (seventeen-and-a-half per cent each), then (assuming that the other parties put up only one candidate each) it will fail to win a seat in spite of having the largest number of supporters.

Here is an actual example from the 1979 House of Representatives election. In Nagano No 3 constituency, which returned four members, the JSP endorsed two candidates, one a sitting member. The result was:

Candidate	Vote	Result
Independent (1)	60,093	Elected
LDP (1)	52,865	Elected
LDP (2)	50,865	Elected
JCP	50,837	Elected
LDP (3)	48,694	Not elected
JSP (1)	35,453	Not elected
JSP (2)	25,748	Not elected
Independent (2)	18,579	Not elected

By putting up two candidates and splitting its vote, the JSP lost the seat it had held in that constituency for over twenty years. In 1980, the party again endorsed only one candidate and regained its seat.

Not all of those who wish to stand as candidates of a particular party therefore are able to obtain endorsement. At every election a considerable number of such people stand anyway, as independents, and usually a dozen or so win seats. On entering the Diet they join the party for which they had originally hoped to stand. The majority of successful 'independent' candidates in fact are people who have been unable to get endorsement from the LDP; more than half of the 'independents' elected to the House of Representatives between 1960 and 1979 were later to be found listed in the Diet handbook, *Kokkai Binran*, as LDP members (including, for example, the 'independent' who headed the poll in Nagano No 3 in 1979).

The parties have become extremely skilful at calculating their strength in each constituency; in the 1980 election eighty-five per cent of candidates for the House of Representatives endorsed by the LDP and JSP were elected. The total number of candidates is nowadays usually less than twice the number of seats. (In 1980, for example, there were 835 candidates for the 511 seats in the House of Representatives.) Relatively few votes are 'wasted'.

The same considerations must be taken into account in organising the campaign. Take the example of a constituency in which the Kōmeitō, say, has enough support to win two seats. If it endorses two candidates, who both campaign throughout the constituency, one may prove to be more popular than the other, win almost all the Kōmeitō votes, and deprive his colleague of a seat. Candidates for the same party therefore usually divide the constituency up, each campaigning in only one part of it. The party's vote is thus spread as evenly as possible.

It should not be thought however that the party organisation is necessarily the most important instrument for gathering votes (as it usually is in Britain). The personal standing of the candidate in the constituency is often of equal or greater importance, especially in the case of LDP candidates, and the solid core of votes that he can rely on is his rather than his party's. Many voters, especially conservatives, claim to vote for the candidate rather than the party. A particular candidate's support may be so firm that he is able to rely on it even when he changes parties; Suzuki Zenkō, who became President of the LDP, and Prime Minister, in July 1980, was first elected to the Diet as a Socialist.

How does the candidate set about building up a support base of this kind? In rural areas, and in local elections, he may rely on the voter's direct or indirect personal knowledge of him; if he is a candidate at all, he is almost certainly a man of some considerable reputation in his locality. But in the cities, and in elections at national level, this is hardly

Addressing a meeting during the 1979 General Election campaign.

possible; there are simply too many voters. So there has arisen, since the late 1950s, as a kind of transitional device between the old rural society, with its network of personal relationships, and the impersonal modern industrial city, the politician's *kōenkai* – the 'personal support group' or supporters' club. The functions of the *kōenkai* are to nurture support for the politician in his constituency (including organising his 'surgeries' when he comes down from Tokyo) and to run his campaign at election time, setting up his election headquarters, dealing with election officials, the police and the press, putting up posters, canvassing, and so on. Masumi Junnosuke describes a Sunday morning in the office of the *kōenkai* of an LDP Dietman: 'By seven o'clock there are twenty people waiting, drinking tea and talking quietly, in the twelve-foot-square front room, all in their best clothes. Their occupations are various: timber merchant, local assemblyman, cobbler, teacher, horse-coper. The Secretary, a dwarfish old man, calls them out one after another and conducts them into a little room overlooking the back garden. There sits the member . . . at a large low table. He listens and takes notes, then scribbles a few words on one of his visiting cards, saying something like, "If you take this with you, I expect they'll see you right about the tobacconist's licence". . . . After he has seen several dozen people, off he goes, following the Secretary's crowded schedule for the day, to a wedding, to a topping out ceremony, to visit a sick person'.

A Diet member's *kōenkai* is often a surprisingly large organisation. In the early 1970s for example, Nakasone Yasuhiro's *kōenkai*, which was organised into seven 'federations', with chapters in the various towns and villages of the constituency, had about 50,000 members. Ten per cent of the Japanese population were said to belong to the *kōenkai* of LDP Diet members at that time. Many *kōenkai* officers are themselves local politicians, who are thus connected upwards with a particular Diet member and themselves carry the connection downwards, often through *kōenkai* of their own, to the grass roots.

Election campaigning in Japan is hedged about with numerous restrictions. These were imposed originally in 1925, when the Manhood Suffrage Act was passed, as a means of regulating the political activities of the newly enfranchised working class. They have been retained largely as a means of reducing corruption, but are so numerous – and some of them so seemingly arbitrary – that they are virtually impossible to observe. As well as forbidding 'treating' and gifts to supporters, the regulations ban signature-drives, the publication of the results of opinion polls immediately before an election and door-to-door canvassing. Limits are placed on the number of motor vehicles that may be used and on the size and number of posters and where they may be displayed. Only a certain number of speech meetings may be held, only at certain times, and only certain people may speak at them.

Many of these regulations are ignored. Gifts of food and drink are such an integral part of Japanese social life that a ban on them is simply impracticable. The ban on house-to-house canvassing is also virtually impossible to enforce. (Although for those who are convicted, the penalty can be severe; in October 1979 a Borough Councillor in Tokyo was fined ¥100,000 and deprived of his civil rights for two years for visiting voters' homes to solicit their votes. On a number of occasions, inferior courts have ruled that this prohibition violates Article 21 of the Constitution, which guarantees freedom of speech, but the Supreme Court has declined to uphold these judgments.)

There is much corruption in Japanese politics, and after every election there are numerous prosecutions for serious offences. In the month following the 1979 House of Representatives election the police investigated over 7,000 cases of suspected violations of the election law, involving more than 13,000 people; over 6,000 of these cases were instances of suspected vote-buying. The National Police Agency estimated that ¥200,000,000 (or an average of a little over ¥3,000 a vote) had been spent for this purpose. One candidate indeed, who failed to win a seat, was thought to have spent over ¥15,000,000. It is this practice in particular that the ban on house-to-house canvassing is designed to discourage.

Factionalism

The LDP and the JSP are both, to use a cliché often applied to the British Labour Party, 'coalitions of factions'. We may define a 'faction' as a section of a party that has, to a greater or lesser extent, separated itself from the party as a whole in order to pursue particular ends: the promotion of some policy or strategy not yet accepted by other sections of the party, perhaps, or the advancement of one of its members to the party leadership. Groups of this kind are familiar enough in European and American politics. Why then is so much attention paid to them by commentators on Japanese politics?

The answer is that party 'factions' in Japan are much longer-lived and more highly organised, much less *ad hoc*, than their Western counterparts. In the LDP they are fundamental to the structure of the party, and compete with each other for funds and votes in a way that is unknown in Britain. It would not perhaps be going too far to suggest that in Japan there are eight or ten separate conservative *parties*, which form coalition governments, normally vote together in the Diet, and campaign under the same banner in general elections.

In one sense, the faction is a traditional leader-follower group based on personal relationships of a kind that is found throughout Japanese society – in, for example, business circles, government ministries, and the academic and artistic worlds. An important benefit for members of such groups is the very sense of membership, of belonging. But this is not the only, nor even the most important, reason why Japanese politicians organise themselves into factions. If these groups arose simply because of the nature of traditional Japanese society, we should expect to find that they were more firmly entrenched in the pre-war than in the post-war parties. But the reverse is true. Factions certainly existed in the pre-war parties, but their absolute domination of conservative politics is a post-war phenomenon.

The existence of factions is generally deplored, even by conservative politicians, partly because they lead to corruption and rumours of corruption, and partly because they are seen as 'un-modern'. LDP politicians, including Prime Ministers, frequently exhort one another to disband their factions, in the name of 'party modernisation', and from time to time the deed is actually done. But sooner or later the monsters come lumbering out of the swamp again to drip mud and weeds on the floors of the Diet and the expensive restaurants where the wheeling and dealing is done.

It is generally agreed that the most important role in keeping factions alive is played by the electoral system, which forces members of the same party to compete for votes. For example, in a constituency which returns five members to the House of Representatives, the LDP may calculate that it has enough support to win three seats. It therefore endorses three candidates, each of whom must attempt to persuade as many voters as possible to cast their votes for him. Since a conservative politician must seek to attract the 'conservative' vote, writing off 'progressive' voters, it is with the other candidates of his own party, rather than those of the opposition parties, that he will be competing most directly. Various means have been devised of securing the election of as many of the party's candidates as possible by using the vote in the most efficient way, but the fundamental conflict of interest within the party is inescapable.

The party itself must avoid exacerbating the conflict and so takes as nearly neutral a role as possible. It cannot put more of its campaign resources behind one candidate than behind another, and since its resources are limited, it can offer only very limited support to each. The individual candidate must therefore seek financial and other aid from sources other than the party. He does so by joining one of the intra-party factions, which are highly organised bodies with their own headquarters and administrative staffs. Their leaders have access to funds from a variety of sources. One leader may have had a successful career as an official in the Ministry of Finance before entering politics and have built up relationships in financial circles that now enable him to obtain large donations for political purposes from such organisations as banks; another may have made his fortune in the construction industry; a third may have married into one of the great families of industrialists and receive support from the firms associated with the family.

Huge amounts of money are received by faction leaders. In 1976 the law governing political donations was revised and the reporting of donations made and received is now more strictly controlled. For this and other reasons the role of factions in gathering funds may have been somewhat modified, and money may now be donated more frequently to individual Diet members. But it remains true that the factions command larger funds than the party's central fund-raising organisation, and it is generally acknowledged that a good deal more money actually passes through their coffers than is reported.

Much of this money is distributed by the faction leader to his followers. (What he principally receives in return is their support in his jockeying for position and bargaining for power with other faction leaders.) The money is used by the faction members partly for office expenses and partly for 'nursing' their constituencies, building up the support that will ensure their re-election. It is an expensive business. We may form some idea of how much money is spent, and for what purposes, from an interview with four LDP Dietmen which was published in the *Asahi Shinbun* on 2 July 1975. One of them was Katō Kōichi, who sits for Yamagata No 2 Constituency.

Katō received at the time a Diet member's salary of ¥650,000 a month and an expenses allowance (for correspondence, travel, etc.) of ¥350,000 a month. The salaries of two secretaries (totalling ¥358,000 a month) were paid on his behalf from official funds. His monthly expenditure however averaged ¥1,800,000. His Tokyo office cost ¥600,000 a month to run, and he spent ¥900,000 a month on his constituency. His personal living expenses came to ¥300,000.

The money spent on his constituency was used for a variety of purposes. The largest single item was the cost of running his *kōenkai*, but gifts of congratulation or condolence to constituents, donations of various kinds (a mirror for the new public hall, trophies for sports meetings and fishing competitions), and greetings cards at new year and in the summer season cost considerable sums. He was also expected to contribute about half the cost of trips to Tokyo for parties of constituents to visit the Diet.

Where did the extra money come from? Katō received about ¥8,000,000 a year from a support group set up in Tokyo by businessmen from his constituency, ¥6,000,000 from small businesses and individuals in his constituency, and ¥2,000,000 to ¥3,000,000 from his faction. (Katō belonged to the Ōhira faction, whose leader, Ōhira Masayoshi, was Prime Minister from December 1978 until his death in June 1980.)

The four Dietmen interviewed all agreed that contributions from big business could cause ethical difficulties. Katō remarked that a gift of ¥10,000 from a small firm in your constituency was harmless – it was merely a gesture equivalent to saying 'go out and win the championship' to your favourite wrestler; but contributions from firms or associations powerful enough to have an influence on government or ruling-party policy were a problem. It was agreed however that under the present constituency system, which obliged you to compete more fiercely with your conservative colleagues than with the candidates of opposing parties, it would be very difficult to do without these contributions. Katō also commented that the voters who criticised 'money politics' should realise that if they expected to receive a wreath and a condolence gift from their Diet member when a relative died, or a garland of flowers when they opened a new shop, then they must accept the need for him to get the money from somewhere.

The critics of factionalism (and there are none more vociferous than the politicians themselves) believe that if factions could be eliminated the parties would become 'modern'. But behind the practical, financial reasons for the survival of these bodies there lies an important social factor: the strong Japanese preference for working (in almost all spheres) through informal personal relations. What is seen as the 'unmodern', diffused and *ad hoc* nature of Japanese parties would be likely to survive even the abolition of factions. The factions of the LDP indeed *were* disbanded in the spring of 1977, but it was not long before they reappeared. What prompted their re-emergence was the prospect of an election, under new rules, for the party Presidency. The dissolution of factions and the new system of electing the President were two of the five points of party modernisation adopted at the LDP Congress of April 1977, and it is ironical that the new election system should, in the event, have had the effect of reviving the factions, and even of making them more respectable.

Counting the ballot papers after the voting in the LDP Party Presidential election of November 1978.

Under the old system the President was elected by the LDP Diet members and representatives of each of the prefectural LDP Associations. Under the new system there was to be a primary election, in which all party members would have a vote, to choose two candidates who would go forward to a final election in which only the LDP Diet members would vote. The immediate result was that all the factions began to recruit new members to the party as fast as possible, often paying the membership subscription for them. (The assumption was that most, at any rate, of the new members recruited through the efforts of a particular faction would vote in the primary election for the candidate supported by that faction.)

In January 1978 the membership of the LDP stood at about 800,000, but from the beginning of February the number began to rise by 10,000–20,000 a day and by the end of the month had reached about 1,250,000. It was not only the factions whose leaders were candidates in the primary that were active in recruiting new members. Those without a candidate realised that it was important for them to be seen to be able to have some influence on the outcome; if they played a negligible role in the election, their bargaining position in any future distribution of posts and patronage would be weakened. The individual Diet members too, since the primary election would reveal the strength of their personal following in the party at prefectural level, needed to enlist as many supporters as possible in the party's ranks.

Most new members were recruited not directly by the Diet members themselves but by city and prefectural assemblymen, most of whom have ties with individual Diet members. The effect of the new system was therefore to *strengthen* factionalism in the party by enabling it to penetrate to the grass-roots. Formerly it had been restricted to Diet members and local assembly-men; the rank-and-file supporters of the party had been affected by it only indirectly. Now large numbers were drawn into the party by the factions, and the line of association was extended from the faction leader through the individual Diet member to the prefectural assemblymen, the city assemblyman and the ordinary party member.

The first election under the new system was held in November 1978. There were four candidates – Fukuda Takeo, the incumbent President and Prime Minister; Ōhira Masayoshi, the Secretary-General of the party organisation; Kōmoto Toshio, the Minister for International Trade and Industry; and Nakasone Yasuhiro, a former Cabinet Minister and Secretary-General. All except Kōmoto Toshio were the leaders of powerful factions; Kōmoto stood as the representative of a fourth large faction in the Party. It was generally predicted that the highest vote in both the primary and the run-off elections would go to Fukuda. Indeed Fukuda was himself so confident of his ability to win the primary that he proposed that the candidate who came second should withdraw from the run-off. He was hoist with his own petard; Ōhira won the primary with a handsome majority, and Fukuda himself was obliged to bow out. There was considerable anger among the members of the Fukuda faction. In particular, they resented the part played in their leader's defeat by Tanaka Kakuei, the leader of a powerful faction which had not put up its own candidate.

To understand the complex relationships among the various factions, which have shaped the character of the LDP in the 1970s, it is necessary

Ōhira Masayoshi gives a press conference after his victory in the LDP Party Presidential election of November 1978.

to go back to 1972 when Satō Eisaku, who had been Prime Minister since 1964, decided to retire. Fukuda had long been a close associate of Satō's and was generally regarded as his 'heir apparent'. It was Tanaka however, a self-made millionaire not noted for the delicacy of his political conduct, who won the contest to succeed Satō. Accusations were made against him of foul play, including large-scale bribery. Tanaka was Prime Minister for only two years; in 1974, he was forced to resign as a result of a scandal over his finances. On this occasion too Fukuda was unable to gain enough support to win the LDP Presidency, which went in the end to Miki Takeo, a compromise candidate, and something of a maverick in LDP terms. Miki made himself unpopular with the party's leaders by refusing to hold back in investigating the Lockheed scandal, and after the party's poor showing in the 1976 election he was forced to resign.

In 1976 Fukuda at last became President of the LDP, but when he was defeated in the 1978 Presidential Election his supporters alleged that Tanaka's faction, which had supported Ōhira, had fought a 'dirty' campaign. Ōhira had to form his cabinet amidst rancour and recrimination, which came to a head when he proposed Suzuki Zenkō for the post of Secretary-General of the party. This is the second most powerful office in the LDP, and Fukuda's followers maintained that an 'understanding' had been reached in 1974 that it should not be held by a member of the President's own faction. They objected particularly strongly to Suzuki because of his close connections with Tanaka. Ōhira proposed instead another member of his own faction to whom it seemed likely that Fukuda's followers would take less violent exception. Fukuda himself agreed to this proposal, but several intransigent members of his faction threatened not to attend the special Diet session at which Ōhira would be elected Prime Minister. Only a small number of abstentions by LDP members was needed to rob Ōhira of his majority. Unwilling to risk humiliation, he put off the special Diet session until the next day, the first time for nearly twenty years that such a vote had been postponed. Eventually the disaffected members of the Fukuda faction were persuaded to vote in return for a promise that a special office would be set up to promote party reform and to look into 'money politics'.

Within a year of becoming Prime Minister Ōhira decided to call an election. The LDP's majority in both Houses of the Diet had been reduced to a bare minimum at the elections of 1976 and 1977, but by 1979 there were reasons to think that it might be possible for the party to achieve once again the kind of 'stable majority' it had enjoyed in the 1960s. In the local elections of 1979, a number of prefectures and big cities had replaced 'progressive' governors and mayors with conservatives, and public opinion polls seemed to confirm this conservative revival.

In the event, although the LDP increased its share of the vote at the 1979 election, it was unable to increase its representation in the diet –

largely, it seems, because factional disagreements led the party to put up too many candidates in a number of seats which they might otherwise have won. The Fukuda and Miki factions put a great deal of pressure on Ōhira to 'take responsibility' for the poor result by resigning. Ōhira refused. The struggle continued for over a month after the election. Eventually, Fukuda took the unprecedented step of standing against Ōhira in the Diet election for Prime Minister. Ōhira won narrowly. This did not end the long-standing feud between the two men however; in May 1980, when the JSP (with little hope of success) moved a vote of no confidence in the Ōhira cabinet, the Fukuda and Miki factions abstained from voting, thus bringing the Government down. Fukuda and Miki had expected, no doubt, that Ōhira would resign the party Presidency, but instead he dissolved the House of Representatives and called an election, to be held (for the first time) on the same day as the House of Councillors' election that was already due. In the middle of the campaign, Ōhira died of a heart attack.

The result of the election was a landslide victory for the LDP, which won a bigger share of the vote than at any general election since 1967, a

Suzuki Zenko, the Japanese Prime Minister, with his cabinet after the LDPs landslide victory in the General Election of June 1980.

higher proportion of the seats in the House of Representatives than at any election since 1969 and more seats in the House of Councillors than at any election since 1968. Ōhira's death seems to have been one reason for the LDP's success, but the most important reason for the big swing back to the ruling party appears to have been that the Japanese voter had no confidence in the opposition parties' capacity to provide a satisfactory alternative Government; he voted therefore for the stability and continuity which the LDP seemed likely to provide.

After the election, there was another contest for the party leadership. Finally, Suzuki Zenkō, whose nomination as Secretary-General of the LDP in 1978 had so angered the Fukuda faction, and who had succeeded to the leadership of the Ōhira faction, emerged as a compromise President – largely because he managed to secure the support of both the Tanaka and the Fukuda factions. Suzuki, who has the reputation of a first-class behind-the-scenes negotiator, announced that he would pursue the politics of 'compromise and reconciliation'. Though, once again, the factions were officially disbanded during the contest, the events of this election confirmed (if any confirmation were needed) that, in spite of all the efforts to eradicate it, factionalism is still firmly rooted in the LDP.

Conclusion

Japanese democracy, like that of every other 'democratic' country, is highly imperfect. It is shaped, as we have seen, by social and other factors that are peculiar to Japan; and it is tempered, like that of every other 'democratic' country, with money and privilege (with more money and less privilege perhaps than Britain's). But it is clear that Japan does now belong to the small class of 'parliamentary democracies'; it is one of the few countries, that is, of which it is possible to say – without a complete disregard for the meaning of words – that a well-educated electorate, comprising four-fifths of the population, informed by a free press, regularly exercises in free elections the right to choose the members of the sole law-making organ of the state. In a narrow sense it has been possible to say this of Japan since 1946, but it is perhaps only in the last decade that Japanese democracy has become truly 'parliamentary'. After the turbulence of the first post war decade, the LDP was for fifteen years secure enough in the seat of power to ride roughshod, when it wished, over the opposition parties. The frustration of the opposition in the face of this conduct led on many occasions to violent disturbances within the Diet. It was common (especially after the large-scale riots over the Security Treaty in 1960) to speak of an 'extra-parliamentary' opposition. During the 1970s however negotiation and compromise came nearer to being the parliamentary norm. Political violence has become rare both in the Diet and in the streets. (Almost the only issue that has led to riots of a kind common in the 1960s has been the construction of the new Tokyo Airport at Narita – a project that had been conceived and pushed through during that decade).

The world is not a safe place for democracy, and Japan's, although in times of prosperity robust enough, is as vulnerable as any other to, say, an economic disaster. But, barring such a disaster, there is no reason to think that democracy is in any greater danger in Japan than elsewhere.

6
Japan in the World
Gordon Daniels

Introduction

Ever since the creation of the modern Japanese state in 1868 its foreign policy has been based partly on national tradition and partly on the desire to play a significant role in the world. In the nineteenth century Japan's new leaders studied Western diplomacy in order to protect the nation's culture and independence, and within twenty years they had mastered the subtleties of negotiation and international law. By 1914, like any other modern power, Japan had colonies, spheres of influence, and an alliance with Britain; and at the end of the First World War she joined the victors in shaping the pattern of the post-war world. During these fifty years of modernisation Japan's diplomats came to share many of the values of their Western counterparts but, unlike the ambassadors of European states, they were often bitterly condemned by public opinion. Many Japanese disliked the compromise of national interest involved in diplomatic negotiation, while others wanted Japan to liberate the rest of Asia from the imperialist West. This kind of pan-Asian patriotism had little influence until the 1930's, when it provided the propaganda basis for Japan's expansionist policies, but by 1945 Japan's defeat had again restored the West to a central place in her political consciousness.

During the occupation the United States was the model for the country's post-war social reconstruction and friendship with America became the dominant concern of Japanese foreign policy. Washington established close links with Japanese political leaders, supplied financial aid for her economic recovery, and provided the armed forces for her defence. Most important of all, the implicit alliance between America and Japan was further strengthened by the commitment to a common ideology. In the post-war years Japan was dominated by conservative leaders who favoured free enterprise and abhorred Communism, and Soviet behaviour appeared to confirm their anti-Communist views. In August 1945 Stalin had declared war on Japan to profit from her destruction, and even after the country had surrendered the Red Army occupied South Sakhalin and the Kurile islands (see the map on page 190). Later still, Russian ill-treatment of Japanese prisoners further alienated public opinion.

On 8 September 1951 forty-nine powers—including the United States and Great Britain – signed a peace treaty with Japan at San Francisco. Both the People's Republic of China and the Soviet Union rejected it, however, because they objected to the freedom which the new peace provided for Japanese rearmament. The treaty exacted no reparations and placed no restrictions on Japanese trade and industry, but Japan's independence was far from complete. America continued to administer the strategic Bonin and Ryūkyū islands (which lie to the south of Japan), and her diplomatic influence compelled Japan to ignore Peking and recognise the government of Nationalist China in Taipei.

Parallel with the peace treaty Japan and the United States signed a security pact which provided that America 'should maintain armed forces of its own in and around Japan so as to deter armed attack' and 'put down large scale internal riots and disturbances . . . caused by an outside power'. After Japan's defeat the allies had dissolved Japan's armed forces and compelled her to accept a constitution Article 9 of which renounced war 'as a sovereign right of the nation' and declared that 'land, sea and air forces . . . will never be maintained'. However, when Communist North Korea invaded South Korea in June 1950 the American occupation authorities were afraid of Communist subversion in Japan and authorised the creation of a paramilitary National Police Reserve. In 1951 the United States, which was deeply afraid of Communist aggression in East Asia, urged Japan to expand this lightly armed force of 75,000 men into a professional army of 300,000. But public opinion was overwhelmingly hostile to rearmament, and Prime Minister Yoshida rejected these demands. As a result, when Japan regained her sovereignty in April 1952, 260,000 United States forces remained on her soil.

Japan and the United States 1952 to 1971

In the 1950s, therefore, the first task of Japanese diplomats was to construct a more equal relationship with the United States. Events outside Japan gave them considerable assistance in achieving this. In 1953 the Korean War ended and the United States was able to withdraw considerable forces from the Far East. As a result by 1959 only 65,000 American troops remained in Japanese bases. In 1952 Japan's National Police Reserve was renamed the National Safety Force, and in 1954 the

Safety Forces were re-organised as the Ground, Maritime, and Air Self-Defense Forces with a strength of 214,000 men. In 1957 a Joint Japanese-American Committee on Security was established to give the Japanese greater influence in high-level military consultations, and on 19 January 1960 a new Treaty of Mutual Co-operation and Security was signed in Washington. This ended America's right to suppress internal disorder in Japan, provided for more frequent consultations, and placed a ten-year limit on the new agreement. To many Japanese, however, their Government appeared more concerned to preserve the military partnership with the United States than to protect the interests of their own citizens. On both right and left there was subconscious resentment at Japan's political weakness, but the country's conservative leaders saw no practical alternative to a close association with the United States.

In the years that followed, commercial antagonisms created the first serious conflict in Japanese–American relations. At first, since both President Kennedy and Prime Minister Ikeda Hayato believed that their countries might suffer from the protectionism of the European Economic Community, the two countries seemed to share the same economic interests, and in 1961 this led to the creation of a Joint Trade and Economic Affairs Committee. In the early 1960s the United States still had a favourable trade balance with Japan but she was already alarmed at the effect of Japanese textile imports on her domestic industry. By 1965 the balance of trade had been reversed, Japan had achieved a surplus, and a United States representative declared that 'relations with Japan had more of an adverse impact on America's financial situation than relations with any other single country in the world'. Americans continued to be disturbed at the success of Japanese textile exports, and though they gained no more than seven per cent of the United States market they acquired a symbolic importance out of all proportion to their economic significance. In March 1971 the Japanese textile industry promised a three-year limit on increases in exports, but American companies were far from satisfied. Finally, on 15 August 1971, President Nixon placed a ten per cent surcharge on all foreign imports. Within two months Japan agreed to further restrictions. Confronted by this 'Nixon shock' the Japanese, who believed that they had made substantial concessions, felt deeply wounded by what they saw as the first insensitive act in a close and harmonious partnership.

In spite of the publicity which surrounded the textile controversy Japan gave loyal and devoted support to America's policy in Vietnam while the United States showed increasing sensitivity to Japan's demands for the return of the Ryūkyū and the Bonin islands. In 1965, when Prime Minister Satō requested the return of the Ryūkyūs, President Johnson immediately promised the transfer of the less important Bonin islands. Four years later the United States agreed to begin negotiations for the

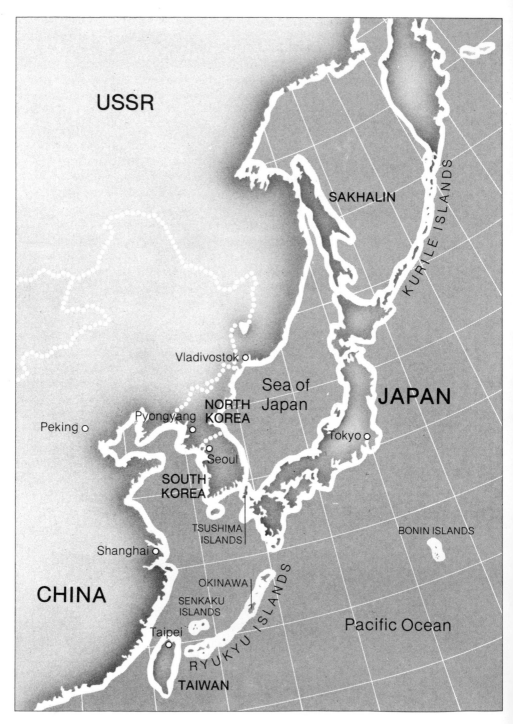

Ryūkyūs' return. On 15 May 1972 the islands were finally transferred to Japanese administration and all territorial disputes between Tokyo and Washington were at an end.

Japan and the Soviet Union 1952 to 1971

In contrast to the mature flexibility of American–Japanese co-operation, Japan's relations with the other great super-power, the Soviet Union, remained harsh and antagonistic. In the 1950's this hostile atmosphere was particularly evident in Soviet fishing policy. Moscow refused Japanese vessels access to many of their traditional fishing grounds, a number of fishing boats were seized and, in the absence of diplomatic relations, redress was difficult and sometimes impossible. Eventually, in 1955, negotiations began on all outstanding issues, but Japan approached them from a position of weakness. She sought the return of her prisoners of war, help in gaining admission to the United Nations, long-term fishery agreements, and the return of the territories occupied by the Soviet Union in 1945. Unfortunately she could offer little in return except the opening of a Soviet Embassy in Tokyo. In the event Japan was compelled to abandon any serious claim to South Sakhalin and the Kuriles, while Russia refused to concede anything except the two coastal islands, Habomai and Shikotan (see the map on page 6). There was total deadlock over Japan's claim to the islands of Etorofu and Kunashiri and the negotiations ended in October 1956 with no more than a formal Joint Declaration.

This ended the state of war between the two parties, reopened diplomatic relations and provided a framework for future discussion. The Soviet Union also agreed to support Japan's application for membership of the United Nations, to return her prisoners of war and to sign a ten-year fishing convention covering the North West Pacific, but a full peace treaty appeared to be unattainable.

These negotiations merely confirmed Japan's traditional suspicions of her northern neighbour, and later relations continued in a similar vein. There were cultural exchanges and visits by official delegations but the professions of mutual friendship which were made on such occasions were no more than a hollow ritual. Soviet patrol boats still seized Japanese fishing vessels, and crews were cynically released to commemorate the anniversary of the Bolshevik revolution. When talks about fishing rights were held Soviet representatives often prolonged them until the eve of the new season so that the Japanese were forced to accept unfavourable terms. As the cold war eased, however, trade began to expand and towards the end of the 1960s there were marked improvements in economic relations. In 1968 Japan undertook to provide $133 millions-worth of equipment to assist timber projects on the Amur river, but optimistic ideas of substantial Japanese exports or of cheap raw materials from Siberia always exceeded commercial realities. And Japan's fundamental suspicion of the Soviet Union remained.

Japan and China 1952 to 1971

Relations with Japan's largest neighbour, China, have always been far more complex. Many Japanese have always felt a cultural debt to China for its great contribution to their own civilisation, but in the twentieth century Japan's military and industrial successes produced a feeling of racial superiority which culminated in Japan's invasion and conquest of China in the 1930s. In the post-war years a new generation of Japanese felt guilt for their country's wartime misdeeds, while many journalists and scholars sympathised with the social ideals of the Communist régime in Peking. Before the Second World War China had been responsible for a quarter of Japan's trade, but after 1945 the allied occupation and the Chinese civil war prevented the resumption of this valuable commerce. After Peking's intervention in the Korean War Washington discouraged the growth of Sino-Japanese trade. The United States had already refused to recognise the Chinese Communist régime, and in 1952 Japan signed a Peace Treaty with Chang Kai-shek's Nationalist régime on Formosa.

Nevertheless, it would be too simplistic to see Japanese policy as merely the result of American compulsion. Chiang Kai-shek had treated Japanese prisoners of war with great humanity, and Japanese conservatives disliked the ideology of the Chinese mainland. Furthermore, Japan's post-colonial connection with Taiwan gave her economic and emotional links with the Nationalist régime which were of great importance. Certainly Japanese socialists and communists who sympathised ideologically with Peking and resented American dominance would have preferred a more independent China policy. But even among conservative businessmen and politicians there were always elements who favoured closer links with Peking. The mainland appeared to offer great trading opportunities and it seemed dangerous to ignore such a powerful neighbour. As a result the China issue was always important in Japanese domestic politics.

During the 1950s, commercial relations with Communist China were largely unofficial and trade with Taiwan remained much more valuable than that with the mainland. In 1960 a new framework was established in which so-called 'friendly firms' – those who had accepted the régime's political principles – were allowed to begin trade with Peking. In 1962 a further unofficial trade agreement – the Li-Takasaki memorandum – was signed. This specified the types and quantities of goods to be exchanged, and established a liaison council to supervise the new trade.

This was a small step in the direction of more formal relations with Peking, but Chiang Kai-shek's hostile reaction soon obstructed further growth. In the late 1960s the Cultural Revolution further damaged Sino-Japanese relations. Peking attacked Japan with strident propaganda, Japanese journalists were expelled, and Prime Minister Satō became the object of particularly hostile criticism on account of his deep anti-communist beliefs and pro-American policies. Twenty years after the San Francisco treaty, Japan remained dependent on Washington and initiatives in China policy were left to the United States.

Japan and South-East Asia 1952 to 1971

Japan's relations with South-East Asia were also fraught with economic and political difficulties. As in China, there were widespread memories of military occupation, though some local leaders had collaborated with the Japanese. But most rulers in South-East Asia were wary of their more powerful neighbour and Japanese attitudes often justified their fears. Japan's sense of cultural superiority damaged many delicate relationships and her preference for dealings with affluent Western nations scarcely commended her to the one-time victims of European rule. Economic relations also provoked much hostility. In 1952 Japan began discussions with Indonesia and the Philippines on the payment of war reparations and these bitter negotiations continued for six years. But reparations were far from being a damaging blow to the Japanese economy. Payments were made in plant, goods, and services, which provided orders for Japanese industry and formed the foundations of future trade.

Political links with South-East Asia were slower to develop. Several Japanese Prime Ministers visited the region; but most countries in the area remained suspicious of Japanese intentions. In the 1960s Japanese industrialists increasingly saw the region as a source of raw materials and useful trade. In most South-East Asian countries they were primarily interested in extracting resources for their own factories and economic 'aid' was often no more than private investment. In Indonesia Japan's wartime co-operation with Sukarno (who became President in 1949) gave her some economic advantages, and the President's marriage to a Japanese beauty cemented a remarkable relationship between the two Governments. After Sukarno's fall in 1966, the appearance of a new military government in Djakarta provided a more stable base for Japan's South-East Asian diplomacy.

Nevertheless, suspicion of Japan continued as aggressive salesmen trampled on local sensibilities, and in Thailand anti-Japanese feeling reached the proportions of a major movement. Japan responded to this unpopularity with more broadly based economic and cultural policies. In 1966 she played a leading role in the creation of the Asian Development

Bank. Technical assistance programmes were gradually expanded, and exchanges of scholars and journalists improved intellectual links with her southern neighbours.

By 1970 there was increasing talk of a distinctive Japanese role in Asia, but the overwhelmingly economic motives of most Japanese activities made the establishment of any true understanding extremely difficult to achieve.

Japan and the United States since 1971

The years from the restoration of Japanese independence in 1952 until 1971 formed a distinct period in the development of Japan's foreign relations. In these two decades Japan's military security was guaranteed by the United States, but the growth of her own forces reduced American bases – which could otherwise have become a major source of friction – to a minor feature in her domestic landscape. During the same period Japan had become a major economic power; her prosperity had been based upon a free flow of fuel and raw materials, and especially on the country's capacity to go on increasing its exports throughout the non-Communist world. The United States in particular provided a market for some thirty per cent of Japanese exports and supplied a similar percentage of her imported goods. But by 1971 several new factors had emerged which endangered the foundations of the country's political and economic security.

Firstly, America's defeat in Vietnam cast doubts upon her ability to protect her allies from a Communist take-over. Similarly, the growing weakness of the American economy, which stemmed in part from the immense financial sacrifices of the Indo-China war, provoked protectionist sentiment in the United States which threatened the Japanese assumption that American markets would always remain open. Even more dramatic from Japan's viewpoint was the sudden change in America's attitude towards China. For twenty years Japan had meekly echoed American hostility to the Peking Government. Now President Nixon took advantage of the Sino-Soviet dispute to improve relations with China and turn the balance of power against the Soviet Union. The sudden revelation of Henry Kissinger's visit to Peking in July 1971 seemed to call into question both America's sincerity and the strength of her alliance with Japan. Although this created embarrassment in Tokyo Japan soon realised the advantages of a more flexible foreign policy – especially the new opportunities for Japanese industry. At the same time both Japan and the United States, taking into account the immense importance of their shared interests, sought to reassure each other of their continuing friendship.

By 1973, the rising value of the yen had done much to slow the threatening rise in Japan's trade surplus with the United States. Nevertheless, economic issues continued to dominate Japanese–American relationships. The Arab oil sanctions imposed after the October war in 1973 for example indicated not only American weakness but the divergent interests of the two allies when resources were in short supply. By 1976 Japan's trade surplus began to increase again and the United States pressed for freer access to the Japanese market for both American agricultural products (such as citrus fruit) and technical equipment (such as computers). The Japanese countered by urging greater efficiency on the Americans. Japan agreed to various voluntary restraints upon her exports, but in dealing with the United States she was often handicapped by deep divisions between different Government departments. Whereas the Japanese Foreign Ministry regarded the alliance with America as all important and favoured compromise, the Ministry of Trade and Industry put economic interests first and resisted American demands. As a result Japanese policies often seemed improvised and inconsistent. In 1978 American pressure finally led Japan to liberalise the import of oranges and American beef. Demands by American companies to be able to sell to Japanese Government agencies also ended in compromise with both sides agreeing, in principle, to allow the other the right to tender for official contracts. Yet the solution of these problems was followed by the emergence of new difficulties. By 1979 imports of small, fuel-saving Japanese cars were leading to unemployment in the American motor industry. Yet even the seriousness of this question did not produce a simple call for protectionism. The President of the American United Auto Workers Union encouraged Japanese manufacturers to avoid putting Americans out of work by building factories in the United States. Such suggestions indicated the desire for compromise, and the fear of a trade war, which existed in both Washington and Tokyo. It seemed that the resilience of the friendship between the two countries could survive a remarkable degree of strain and controversy.

Behind all these material conflicts there still were broader political and military considerations which remained the ultimate determinants of Japanese–American relations. Despite growing scepticism of American strength, Japan remained dependent upon the United States' nuclear umbrella and opposed any American moves to withdraw from nearby areas of strategic importance. After America's final humiliating defeat in Vietnam Japan was concerned that the United States might remove her forces from South Korea; if, as a result, there was a North Korean invasion of the South, this might raise the delicate question of Japanese military assistance to South Korea. In the event, President Carter showed sensitivity to Japanese concern by retaining American air and naval units in South Korea and by delaying his original plans for the removal of all United States' land forces there. Ironically, as America became less willing

The Japanese Prime Minister, Ōhira Masayoshi, with President Carter at the Tokyo Summit meeting, June 1979.

to commit her forces to Asian conflicts, Japan became increasingly concerned to retain as much American power as possible in her immediate vicinity. With the ending of the Vietnam war American bases in Japan – which in any case were further reduced – were no longer a matter of controversy. At the same time the alliance was more widely accepted than ever before, especially since Soviet naval activity in the Far East had become more conspicuous and the potential threat of Soviet power appeared more striking than in the past.

After thirty years of occupation and alliance therefore Japan and the United States remained remarkably close. A relationship of inequality had given way to a more even partnership. Japan remained dependent upon America both as an important market for her exports and as a major source of food and raw materials, but her need for oil and her dependence on overseas trade often led to temporary conflicts with the United States. In 1980 America attempted to organise international sanctions against Iran – to secure the liberation of diplomatic hostages held in the Teheran embassy – but Japan was loath to comply. Iranian oil was not only vital for the Japanese economy but Japan had a large stake in the construction of an immense – and still uncompleted – petrochemical complex. When, as part of her sanctions policy, America refused to buy Iranian oil, Japanese concerns stepped in to purchase it and further friction resulted. This was followed by Japanese expressions of verbal support for the United States and tactful apologies, but the conflict of interests was undeniable. Similarly, when the United States bitterly criticised the Soviet Union for its invasion of Afghanistan, some Japanese sought to escape any deep involvement in the issue. They feared that a worsening of relations with Moscow would damage Japanese trade with the Soviet Union and make the northern territories dispute yet more intractable. But in this instance Japan's anti-Soviet feelings came to dominate her reaction. She tripled aid to Pakistan in support of American policy in the area, and quietly complied with America's request to boycott the Moscow Olympics. In spite of their commercial rivalry, therefore, military and political interests gave the alliance between the two countries a remarkable strength, closeness and flexibility.

Japan and the Soviet Union since 1971

In the aftermath of the Nixon shocks, many Japanese hoped that better relations with Moscow might possibly result from their damaged links with Washington. In addition, the Soviet Union's quarrel with China suggested that she might seek to attract Japan away from a deeper understanding with Peking. In January 1972, the Russian Foreign Minister Andrei Gromyko visited Tokyo and it was agreed that negotiations would begin on the long-awaited peace treaty. In October 1973 Prime Minister Tanaka visited Moscow for a summit meeting and at the end of these talks a joint communiqué referred to the 'settlement of outstanding questions left over since the time of the Second World War'. The Japanese naturally interpreted these to include the unsolved issue of the northern islands, but in this they were to be cruelly disappointed. In all subsequent talks, whether in Moscow or Tokyo, Russian negotiators have adopted a rigid and unyielding stance, claiming that the disputed territories are part of the Kurile islands which the Soviet Union received as the result of wartime agreements. Japan still claims that the four islands off the northern coast of Hokkaido are coastal territories which are historically distinct from the Kurile chain.

Similarly, in the field of economic co-operation bright expectations have been the victims of harsh political and financial realities. The Soviet Union hoped to draw Japanese investment into ambitious schemes for the economic development of her Asian territories; and such plans acquired a new importance in view of worsening relations between China and the USSR. For the Soviet Union, the economic development of the border regions would help to consolidate her political grip on these areas in the face of Chinese pressures. For Japan, the development of energy supplies in the region would lessen her dependence on more distant and politically unstable suppliers. In May 1974 Japan agreed to help finance coal and natural gas developments in South Yakutia, and in the following year United States' companies joined in the development. For Japan this was an ideal arrangement, for not only did it ease the financial burden of the project but it provided political cover should China criticise her participation in the scheme. The worsening atmosphere of Sino–Soviet relations made it increasingly difficult to discuss major economic projects without considering their strategic implications. This was particularly true of Moscow's most ambitious plan, for the development of the Tyumen oilfield. A new source of oil from nearby Siberia was attractive to Japanese businessmen, but Russia's plan to construct a new Baikal–Amur railway rather than an oil pipeline created enormous difficulties. Such a line could clearly be used for military purposes in any war with China, and association with its construction might easily damage Tokyo's new relations with Peking. Japan and the United States consequently refused to participate in the scheme. In this, as in many fields of Soviet–Japanese relations, Tokyo's mistrust of Moscow lay at the heart of their mutual difficulties.

Japanese suspicion of Moscow was also increased by Russian attitudes towards other long-standing issues. Throughout the 1970s, fishing continued to be a source of serious friction between the two powers and Russian moves towards the extension of her fishing limits added further difficulties to their relationship. As in the past, the Soviet Union

Above and right
*Japanese fishing
boats. There have
been constant
difficulties with
the Soviet Union
over alleged
violations of the
Russians' 200 mile
fishing limits.*

continued to seize Japanese fishing boats, to fine and even imprison their crews and to release them as part of its diplomatic strategy. At the same time the increasing importance of fish in Soviet food supplies created further tension. By the mid-1970s large Russian fishing fleets were increasingly active near the Japanese coastline, and this not only raised fears of overfishing but was often accompanied by a careless disregard for Japanese nets and equipment which led to lost catches and costly damage. In December 1976, Russia suddenly declared a 200-mile fishery zone and in subsequent talks reduced both the size of Japanese catches and the permitted areas of operation within this zone. Yet, in recent years, the overwhelming shared interest of Japan and the Soviet Union in fisheries and conservation has led to a growing number of technical agreements, which illustrate their increasing mutual concern for the important fishing grounds of the Northern Pacific.

To a much more limited extent such technical co-operation has had its diplomatic parallels for, somewhat erratically, the Soviet Union has sought to charm or threaten Japan away from too close a relationship with China. Since 1975 Russia has tried to distract Japanese attention from the acrimonious issue of the northern territories, and a peace treaty, by suggesting that the two powers sign a treaty of good neighbourliness and friendship. This proposal has often been accompanied by active public relations programmes by the Soviet Embassy in Tokyo. However, such initiatives have all been rejected by Japanese Ministers and diplomats. Japanese cabinets have made the northern territories such an important issue that compromise is politically impossible. Furthermore, the timing of Soviet overtures – whenever a Sino–Japanese agreement has seemed likely – has exposed the Soviet proposal as a somewhat devious diplomatic ruse. What is more, Soviet attitudes to Japan's friendship with the United States have scarcely been improved by closer Sino–American relations. As a result, Soviet behaviour has at times assumed the threatening posture of the early post-war years. At the end of 1976 the pilot of a Soviet MiG-25 jet fighter landed in Hokkaido and requested political asylum. Japan complied with his request, and allowed the United States Air Force to carry out a detailed examination of the aircraft's highly secret technical equipment. Perhaps understandably, the Soviet Union described this as an unfriendly act, but the stern language used on this occasion clearly revived popular fears of the Soviet Union and exposed the hollowness of Russian talk of friendship or neighbourly relations. In 1979 and 1980 these fears received yet further impetus when Soviet forces on the disputed northern islands were increased and the activities of a Soviet spy ring in the Intelligence unit of the Ground Self Defense Forces were exposed.

Despite these profound differences, trade between Japan and the Soviet Union has continued to grow throughout the 1970s and, in areas which

are not politically sensitive, such as seabed oil exploration, there has been limited co-operation. But, in general, Japanese links with Moscow remain the least changed of all her relationships with the major powers. The territorial issue remains unsolved and the Soviet invasion of Afghanistan has stimulated profound suspicion. Now that trade with China has overtaken that with the Soviet Union even the economic advantages of concessions to Moscow appear far less attractive than at any time since the War.

Japan and China since 1971

If Japanese relations with the Soviet Union have been typified by obvious ill-will, those with the two Chinese states have been characterised by both apprehension and romantic illusion. In the immediate aftermath of the American rapprochement with Peking in 1971, many Japanese feared that they might be the victims of the new relationship, but soon they became aware of the new freedom which stemmed from China's warmth towards the West. For the first time it was possible for Japan to expand commercial links with China without threatening the American alliance, and both politicians and businessmen soon became optimistic about the potential of the Chinese market.

Yet for Japan there were two elements in the new situation which created consternation amongst Government leaders. There still existed a deep political and economic commitment to Taiwan which was threatened by Peking's demand for Japan's acceptance of her claim to the island. The long-standing Sino–Soviet alliance also made Japan somewhat sceptical of the friendlier attitude shown by the People's Republic. What was more, even after Kissinger's secret visit to China, Peking propagandists continued to attack Prime Minister Satō and made it clear that any significant improvement in relations between the two countries would depend upon the appearance of a new leader in Tokyo.

In general, it was far easier for Japanese companies, making appropriate ideological noises, to negotiate new contracts with China than it was for politicians to achieve closer relations. In fact a diplomatic breakthrough was delayed until the summer of 1972 when Prime Minister Tanaka visited Peking and agreed to sever Japan's official links with Taiwan. Though Japan was saved some embarrassment by the fact that the Chinese Nationalists took the initiative in breaking off diplomatic relations, many Japanese Diet members were reluctant to see the end of what had been a politically close and economically profitable relationship. In fact, Peking demanded no more than symbolic acknowledgement of her claim to the island, and trade with Taiwan continued through 'unofficial' organisations which were partly staffed by professional diplomats who were 'on leave'. In many ways Peking showed moderation in her dealings with Prime Minister Tanaka and later Japanese leaders. She renounced all claim to reparations and soon abandoned the acid propaganda of earlier years. In commerce too the complexities of the 1960s gradually gave way to freer arrangements. By 1974 a three-year trade agreement had been signed and the value of trade was rising rapidly.

At the centre of the new relationship were talks on the signing of a Peace and Friendship Treaty which would mark the end of an era of war and establish a thorough foundation for a new relationship. The negotiations were complicated by a symbolic issue of great importance. Peking demanded that a treaty should include an 'anti-hegemony' clause, which was clearly aimed at the Soviet Union and would embarrass Japan in her efforts to resolve her territorial dispute with Moscow. This dilemma was made even more acute by China's advocacy of Japan's case. Finally, in 1976, Foreign Minister Miyazawa explained that China's behaviour was obstructing rather than assisting Japanese demands, and Chinese voices were temporarily stilled. This was just one example of the subtle complexities which affected the developing pattern of Sino–Japanese relations. In many fields Japan was uncertain of the realities which lay behind Chinese statements, while the political turmoil in China which resulted from the deaths of Chou En-lai and Mao Tse-tung

The signing of the Treaty of Peace and Friendship between China and Japan in August 1978 – which was an important symbol of the new relationship between the two countries.

and the overthrow of the 'Gang of Four' made many Japanese uncertain of the long term future of Chinese policy.

In trade, too, anticipations were rarely fulfilled. Exchanges grew, but they remained a small proportion of Japan's worldwide trade, and expectations of substantial oil supplies from China were increasingly disappointed. Quantities failed to meet the optimistic targets set in the negotiations and the high wax content of Chinese oil made it necessary to build special plants to refine it. In 1976 trade as a whole fell, and rival claims to the potentially oil-rich Senkaku Islands seemed to threaten the improvement of Sino-Japanese relations. Finally, it was the establishment of a new, more empirical régime in China, and Japan's frustration with Moscow, which led to a dramatic improvement in their relations. In 1978 China turned to a programme of massive modernisation, and abandoned many of her earlier fears of dependence on foreign powers. Japan agreed to make some concessions in the wording of the long-discussed Peace and Friendship Treaty. In August 1978, a Treaty was signed which contained a fine balance of Chinese and Japanese phraseology. Article II stated that neither power would 'seek hegemony in the Asia-Pacific Region or in any other region and that each is opposed to efforts by any other country . . . to establish such hegemony'. In contrast, Article IV declared that the Treaty 'shall not affect the position of either

Left
*Deng Hsiao Ping,
the Chinese deputy
Prime Minister,
with the former
Japanese Prime
Minister, Fukuda
Takeo, during his
visit to Tokyo in
October 1978 for
the ratification
of the peace treaty.*

Above
*Deng Yingchao,
the head of a
visiting Chinese
parliamentary
delegation, at
the Canon
camera factory.*

contracting party in relations with third countries'. But although its words were carefully judged, the Treaty marked the beginning of a new era in Sino-Japanese relations. It also led to a considerable increase in Japan's contribution to the modernisation of China. Japan was to provide plants, technology, and equipment, with particular emphasis on the development of Chinese oil and coal production. In a world where recession and unemployment threatened increasing barriers to Japanese exports the possibilities of the Chinese market took on immense importance. For the Chinese, Japanese technology was deeply attractive because it would speed industrial modernisation; economic co-operation would deepen political friendship, and both developments would strengthen China against the Soviet Union.

It is true that in 1979 China had begun to question her capacity to pay for some of the most expensive Japanese developments, and she was reluctant to accept some loans at normally competitive rates, but Japan responded by arranging massive government and private loans to help China pay for Japanese machinery. In return, deliveries of Chinese coal and oil would provide Japan with another source of much-needed energy. In human, commercial, and political terms, Sino-Japanese relations had been transformed. Nowhere was this more apparent than in China's attitude to former political problems. In the summer of 1979, for example, Peking declared that the Senkaku islands problem could be solved by the next generation. China's changing ideology, her antipathy to the Soviet Union and the mutual economic interests of the two countries had created the basis for a relationship of unprecedented strength and importance.

Japan and South-East Asia since 1971

In the 1970s the gradual improvement in Japan's relations with China have been paralleled by Tokyo's growing support for the non-Communist states of East and South-East Asia. By 1971 a wide variety of Japanese companies and official agencies were financing economic development in South Korea and in the member states of ASEAN, the Association of South East Asian Nations (Indonesia, Malaysia, the Philippines, Singapore, and Thailand). Yet, as in most of her foreign relations, Japan's priorities were overwhelmingly economic and she sought, as far as possible, to avoid ideology and emphasise commerce in her activities in the area. During the closing years of the Vietnam War, for example, Japan gave substantial assistance to America's allies in Saigon, but she also kept an eye on the future and maintained links with Hanoi by supplying medical aid. Indeed many Japanese companies looked to both Vietnamese states as important potential markets and hoped for a substantial role in the expected reconstruction of war-ravaged Indo-China. However, America's disengagement from Vietnam made Japanese support for non-Communist Governments in South-East Asia increasingly important both for political stability and for economic gain. Inevitably the oil crisis of 1973 made nearby raw materials in Indonesia, Thailand, and Malaysia even more attractive than in the past and Japan's aid programme in the region increased rapidly throughout the 1970s.

In 1974 Prime Minister Tanaka made an extensive tour of South-East Asian capitals. Though this was an indication of Japan's growing economic concern for the area the angry demonstrations which greeted him, especially in Indonesia and Thailand, indicated the continuing heavy-handedness of Japanese businessmen and the obtrusiveness of Japanese products, which easily stirred fears of economic domination. Sensitive Japanese had long been aware of the arrogance of some of their fellow countrymen, but the hostile crowds which abused Prime Minister Tanaka produced a deep and widespread inquest into the ethics, motives and behaviour of Japanese officials and businessmen in the area. As a result the Ministry of Trade and Industry drew up a code of conduct for company representatives and established liaison offices in six South-East Asian cities to provide cultural and social guidance for Japanese traders. Perhaps these enlightened activities had some effect, for anti-Japanese feeling clearly declined in later years. The total collapse of South Vietnam in 1975 also dramatised the threat which a Communist Indo-China might pose to the ASEAN states, and increased the importance of Japanese support for economic development and stability. Soon Indonesian leaders asked openly for aid to rebuff Communism, while the Thai Foreign Minister warmly welcomed Japanese investment activities. Shared economic and strategic interests also produced massive Japanese aid and investment in South Korea.

By 1977 not only had American land forces abandoned Indo-China, but the South East Asia Treaty Organisation had been dissolved, and everywhere in the region non-military methods were seen as the most important means of repelling Vietnamese propaganda or subversion. Japan responded to this new atmosphere, and to South East Asian calls for help, with a major political gesture which confirmed her commitment to supporting her southern neighbours. In August 1977 Foreign Minister Hatoyama, Chief Cabinet Secretary Sonoda, and Prime Minister Fukuda attended a meeting with the heads of the ASEAN Governments in Kuala Lumpur and later made official visits to Singapore, Thailand, the Philippines, and Burma.

In Manila the Japanese Premier enunciated what became known as the Fukuda doctrine, the most vivid presentation of Japan's South-East Asian policy to have been issued since the Second World War. As if to quell any possible fears of a revival of Japanese military power, Fukuda said, 'a Japan which does not pose any threat to neighbour countries either in a military way or in any other way can only be viewed as a stabilising force'. He underlined Japan's commitment to peaceful cooperation and undertook to double Japan's programme of government assistance for industrial projects, for infrastructure development to facilitate industrialisation 'and in areas close to the people's welfare, agriculture, health, and education'. Fukuda also emphasised the need for cultural exchanges and heart-to-heart understanding among the peoples of Japan and South-East Asia. For all its obvious rhetoric, Fukuda's pronouncement indicated a serious attempt to escape from Japan's past image as a rapacious economic power with no interest in the aspirations of less developed nations. Yet despite this clear commitment to her non-Communist neighbours, Fukuda attempted to avoid the blatant ideological commitment which had often been so damaging to American policy in East Asia. He praised ASEAN's desire 'to develop peaceful and mutually beneficial relations with the nations of Indochina' and supported the policy of making further efforts to enlarge areas of understanding and co-operation with these countries on the basis of mutuality of interests. Vietnam's invasion of Cambodia in 1979, however, revived ASEAN's suspicions of Hanoi's ultimate objectives, while her alignment with Moscow pressed Japan into an increasingly close association with her ASEAN neighbours. Japan would prefer an open pattern of trade with every country in South-East Asia, but as long as the Sino-Soviet dispute continues, she will find it difficult to avoid an open political preference for the non-Communist régimes in the area.

Japan and the Middle East

Although the Nixon shocks of 1971 undermined the previous political assumptions behind Japan's foreign policy, the Middle East crisis of 1973 produced far more serious threats to her industrial future. From the 1960s onwards oil from Iran and the Arab states had been of increasing importance to the Japanese economy and some of her ablest leaders were well aware of the growing power of the Organisation of Petroleum Exporting Countries. In the spring of 1973 the Minister of International Trade and Industry, Nakasone Yasuhiro, visited four Middle Eastern states and declared that Japan should pay more attention to economic co-operation with oil producers; but by the autumn Japan's policy had been overtaken by political events. At this time approximately eighty per cent of Japan's oil came from Iran and the Arab world and, having virtually no domestic sources of energy, she was cruelly exposed to the diplomatic pressures of Arab leaders. In the past, as a close ally of the United States, Japan had either been pro-Israeli or neutral in the Middle East dispute. Now, threatened with the loss of her industrial lifeblood, she rapidly adopted a pro-Arab stance. On 22 November the Ministry of Foreign Affairs stated that it would 'reconsider its policy towards Israel' unless 'the latter withdraws from the Arab territory which the Jewish state occupied during the war of 1967'. Japan's new standpoint was sufficient to gain acknowledgement of her 'friendly' status by Arab leaders, but her continuing alarm produced an unprecedented surge of diplomatic activity. Within weeks of adopting her new position Japan despatched three prestigious envoys to Iran, the Middle East, and North Africa to promise loans and technical cooperation in exchange for oil. Japanese private companies followed eagerly in the search for orders and Mitsui, Mitsubishi, and Nippon Steel all became active in the region.

Yet this flurry of activity produced results which were only partially successful. Certainly trade boomed; in 1974 exports were 130 per cent higher than in 1973 and in 1975 rose to $6·07 billion, but Japan was a good deal less skilful in securing contracts for larger scale projects. Many of her initial offers had been made without thought to detailed terms, while rising inflation in Japan deterred some would-be clients from long term contracts. Japan's transport costs also placed her at a disadvantage in comparison with Western European competitors. Furthermore, her experience of the Middle East was limited and her diplomats were inexperienced in giving help to businessmen. But it was the material obstacles which prevented closer economic co-operation; shortages of labour and inadequate transport led to the abandonment of many ambitious schemes.

Japan rarely relaxed in her efforts to improve relations with Middle Eastern countries, but they were increasingly aware of their ability to extract a considerable economic and political price for any concessions to the Japanese. In 1977 a Democratic Socialist Diet member visited Saudi Arabia and was told that oil supplies would depend upon the extent of Japanese economic co-operation and on her influencing Washington to concede important Arab demands. By 1978 the importance of the Middle East was further underlined when Japan's Prime Minister and Foreign Minister both visited the area and promised help. But the Shah's fall and the Soviet invasion of Afghanistan underlined the insecurity of the country's existing oil supplies and drove Japan to pursue two distinct policies. She attempted to maintain as good relations as possible with the new Iranian régime, established Arab states, and the Palestine Liberation Organisation. At the same time she began to look for new sources of energy. Japanese interest in Australian coal has increased, and in the spring of 1980 Prime Minister Ōhira visited Canada to negotiate for coal, and Mexico to try to secure further supplies of oil. Japan still realised the importance of the Middle East but she also recognised that in an unstable world no single region could provide a secure supply of her most vital raw material.

Japan and the European Community

In the same years that the Middle East assumed increasing importance for Japanese foreign policy Western Europe also, and for the first time, became a significant factor in Japan's post-war economic relations. In the immediate aftermath of war links between Japan and Western Europe had been negligible; both concentrated on economic reconstruction and both looked to the United States for economic and military support. Later European leaders, recalling Japan's pre-war pirating of designs and dumping of industrial products, resisted her admission to the General Agreement on Tariffs and Trade. In 1955 Japan was finally permitted to accede to the Agreement, but fourteen countries – including Britain, France, Belgium, and the Netherlands – invoked Article 35 of the treaty which allowed them to continue discriminating against Japanese goods. By 1958 the creation of the European Economic Community seemed to threaten further restrictions against Japanese exporters and Japan began an active programme of ministerial visits aimed at the liberalisation of European attitudes. In 1962 Anglo-Japanese negotiations culminated in a Commercial Treaty and Britain's abandonment of Article 35. Soon France and the Benelux countries followed Britain's example and throughout the 1960s both Japan and Western European countries pursued increasingly liberal policies. In these years mutual trade grew from negligible to significant proportions; by 1970 Japan was exporting $1,303 millions-worth of goods to EEC countries, and a further $1,059 millions-worth to the members of the European Free Trade Association.

As late as 1967 Japan's trade with the EEC was slightly in deficit but during the 1970s a growing Japanese surplus became a recurrent feature of relations between Tokyo and the enlarged European Community.

Throughout the 1960s European leaders had talked of negotiating a commercial treaty with Japan, but mutual disagreements prevented meaningful discussions until 1971, when a general European-Japanese agreement was reached on the desirability of freer trade and the reduction of all forms of commercial protection. But European countries still remained fearful of a sudden inrush of Japanese products and suggested that any formal treaty should provide specific safeguards against such a possibility. Naturally Japanese negotiators feared that they might lose from the acceptance of such a provision and declared that, in any crisis, Article 35 of GATT could be invoked. Failure to agree on the terms of a treaty was understandable. The United States was increasingly disturbed by the effects of Japanese exports on the American economy, and European suspicions were aroused by Japan's tendency to see Europe as an alternative market.

Japan's new emphasis on Europe soon achieved impressive results, for by 1973 her surplus on visible trade with the Community had reached $1,233 million and there seemed no immediate prospect of the balance being restored. The increasing scale of this new problem produced concern in Brussels, and the recession which followed the 1973 oil crisis further added to protectionist sentiment in Western Europe. This growing tension in economic relations generated much diplomatic activity, and high level official consultations began at 'both ministerial level and the level of experts'. As a result specialist negotiations on cars, pharmaceutical goods, silk, iron and steel, ships, agricultural products, chemicals and diesel engines were held with increasing frequency.

As early as 1973 Japan had responded to European unease with voluntary limitations on the export of electronic calculators and steel products to the Community, while similar measures were taken against the export of other products to specific European countries. But as Japan's surplus continued to increase Japanese-EEC relations continued to deteriorate. By 1976 it had reached $3,629 million and, when representatives of the Japanese Confederation of Economic Organisations (Keidanren) visited Brussels, Europeans not only attacked Japan's surplus and the volume of her exports but turned their attention to non-tariff barriers in the Japanese market. These included inspection procedures at points of entry and the complexities of Japan's distribution network.

Viewed from Europe Japan appeared as a dangerous trading partner. Her products had effectively destroyed both the German camera and the British motorcycle industries. Certain Japanese exports, such as cars and ships, had also increased so rapidly that counter-action was extremely difficult and the fear of unemployment created political pressures against

Japanese exports in several European countries. But to the Japanese the situation appeared in very different terms. Although Japanese exports had an undeniable impact on certain European industries their total value was relatively small in proportion to the total imports of the European Community. In 1976 goods from Japan accounted for no more than two per cent of EEC imports. In contrast American products accounted for twelve per cent of European purchases in the same year. Furthermore Europe had a favourable surplus in its invisible trade with Japan which partially offset the much discussed deficit on visible items. To some Japanese it seemed that the Community was returning to the discriminatory attitudes of the 1950s. It made little criticism of imports from the United States and seemed about to protect its inefficient industries with restrictive policies. In addition, European attacks on Japanese tariff and non-tariff barriers appeared to ignore the reduction and simplification of quotas, tariffs and banking regulations which Japan had carried out in the 1960s and 1970s, and the lack of interest in Japanese markets which was apparent in many European companies.

In 1978 Japan announced an emergency import programme which promised some symbolic reduction in her surplus with Europe, but the results of this were singularly disappointing. When European officials attempted to persuade Japan to buy a substantial number of civil aircraft the Japanese Government denied that it had any ability to influence private airlines. And in the spring of 1978 Japanese-EEC relations appeared to reach crisis point. There was deadlock in talks with Tokyo and no agreement on European demands for a speedy simplification of import regulations. At one point Japanese negotiators even questioned the political authority of EEC negotiators, but both parties soon recognised the danger of provocative acts. Japanese leaders suggested that European businessmen should raise loans in Tokyo, a large Japanese import-purchasing mission toured Europe, and a number of import regulations were simplified. Unfortunately Japan's frequent undertakings to reduce her trading surplus went unfulfilled, and despite all her concessions the 1978 surplus reached $5 billion.

In 1979 relations again became acrimonious, particularly when an EEC report branding the Japanese as 'workaholics' was leaked to the press. Yet, as before, Europeans were reluctant to resort to protectionism. Instead they turned to the training of young European executives in Japan as one long-term solution to the problem of exporting to Japan. For their part, Japanese companies sought to ameliorate the surplus problem by increasing investment in European countries. By June 1980 both sides had recognised that heavy handed pressure was no solution to the problem of Japan's rising surplus. Europe and Japan both feared the consequences of a trade war and sought voluntary arrangements and compromises as a solution to their long term difficulties. Any major

change in trade between Japan and Europe will require structural changes in Japan's industry and commerce but a shared consciousness of the importance of their mutual relations may well encourage continued efforts to compromise.

Nike missiles of the Japanese Air Self-Defense Forces on parade.

The Self-Defense Forces

Inevitably the sudden changes in Japan's international position during the 1970s brought a reconsideration of the size and role of her military forces. From the creation of the National Police Reserve at the outset of the Korean War the development of Japan's defence forces has been a subject of the deepest controversy. The strong pacifist feelings of Japanese public opinion compelled every Government to define the role and equipment of Japan's armed forces in strictly defensive terms and on numerous occasions the very legality of their existence has been challenged in the courts. By 1971, after the implementation of three Defense Build-Up Plans, the full complement of 180,000 men for the Ground

Self-Defense Force had still not been achieved; the Maritime force had however acquired seventy-one vessels, most of which were designed for anti-submarine duties, and the Air Self-Defense Force had over 900 aircraft, most of them in interceptor and reconnaisance units.

In 1970, against a background of growing self-confidence and American encouragement, the new director of the Defense Agency, Nakasone Yasuhiro, drew up plans for a further strengthening of all three services. These called for further modernisation and expansion of all armed forces, and Nakasone considered it necessary for Japan to have sufficient power to intercept invaders in international air space and on the high seas. The plans were accepted by the Defense Agency in April 1971 but the Sino-American rapprochement in July the same year removed much of the fear of China which lay behind the scheme. As a result, by the time the National Defense Council finally approved the plan it was drastically reduced. By 1976 Japan's ground forces remained at less than 180,000 men, its naval forces held seventy-five vessels and its airforce 930 aircraft. All were equipped with modern weapons though, according to some commentators, ammunition stocks had fallen and Japan's fighters, for example, had no more than four missiles per aircraft. With the improvement of relations with China, however, the danger of Sino-Soviet military co-operation was eliminated from Japan's defence planning.

On 29 October 1976 the National Defense Council adopted a National Defense Program Outline which approached Japan's military problems from a new standpoint. The outline favoured qualitative as opposed to quantitative improvements in all three forces and abandoned five year build-up programmes in favour of an annual defence review which would allow continuous adjustment to a changing military situation. In line with its emphasis on high quality forces, the new programme called for a defence establishment of overall balance rather than one designed to cope with a specific emergency. This plan was also based upon the idea that major conflict between the great powers was unlikely and that in the immediate future Japan's forces were only to be of a scale to meet 'limited small aggression'. Clearly improved relations with China have been one major influence on defence thinking but by 1979 additional factors had created considerable uncertainty about Japan's military position. In the words of the 1979 Defense White Paper, 'the steady growth of Soviet forces in the Far East is considered to be having an impact on the US–Soviet military balance in the Western Pacific region. The Soviet Union is likewise acquiring a noticeable military potential against the defense of Japan'. Soviet naval forces in North East Asia have improved in both scale and quality and Soviet aircraft frequently approach Japan. In 1978 Soviet aircraft flew close to Japanese air space on over 500 occasions and an infringement of air space led to a Japanese diplomatic protest. In 1979 Soviet forces on the disputed northern islands were also further strengthened and have carried out manoeuvres close to the Japanese coast. In clear response to recent Soviet activities and the invasion of Afghanistan, Japanese defence policies have developed and broadened in several new spheres. Early warning planes have been ordered to supplement land-based radar, new anti-submarine aircraft have been acquired, the submarine fleet has been reorganised and a guard post has been established on Tsushima island between Japan and Korea. Perhaps the most dramatic development has been the increasingly international scope of Japan's defence activities. New defence attachés have been posted to Peking, Vienna, and Oslo, the Director General of the Defense Agency has visited South Korea, Western Europe, and the United States, and in 1979 Self Defense personnel participated with American forces in 'Fortress Gale' exercises in Okinawa. Finally, in February 1980, Japanese naval units joined American, Canadian, Australian, and New Zealand forces in large-scale RIMPAC manoeuvres in the Pacific Ocean.

The Tokyo Summit meeting, June 1979.

All this activity has led to increased concern at the state of Japan's defences and, most important, to a public mood which is more sympathetic to the long-maligned Self Defense Forces – in fact defence has recently emerged as a subject of public discussion in a way that would have been unimaginable only a few years ago. In the early summer of 1978 General Kurisu Hiromi, Chairman of the Joint Staff Council, stated in a published interview that 'in the event of a surprise enemy landing on Japanese soil our hands are tied until such time as the Prime Minister issues orders . . . it is possible that frontline commanders would first take supralegal action'. Such a threat to civilian control led to the General's dismissal and his condemnation by the Director General of Defense, but the Prime Minister also announced that the Defense Agency would study the problems inherent in existing legislation. What is more, discussion of the armed forces in the press and on television has been more open and less emotional than in earlier years – there was, for example, little hostile public reaction to Japan's participation in the RIMPAC exercise. There have also been growing expressions of support for higher defence expenditure, and it seems likely that one per cent of Japan's Gross National Product will soon be devoted to her armed forces. This is unlikely, however, to lead to any crude reversion to the attitudes or policies of the pre-war years. Japanese public opinion remains sceptical of what may be achieved by military power and is opposed to the despatch of forces abroad. The Japanese are also well aware of the suspicion which rapid rearmament could produce overseas. As a result the character of her armed forces is likely to remain fundamentally defensive and, though they may gain more freedom of operation, it is unlikely that the revision of Article 9 of the Constitution would command widespread support.

Conclusion

After more than a century of political and economic modernisation Japan is clearly committed to firm and close relations with North America and Western Europe. Since 1975 her participation in world economic summits has underlined not only her economic importance but her adherence to the broad values of an open society which are shared by Canada, the United States and the European Economic Community. Yet, despite the fundamental importance of Japan's links with Europe and North America, she is dependent upon a much wider world for her continued survival and prosperity. Japan's reliance upon South East Asia, China, Latin America, and Australia for oil, minerals and food, as well as for export markets and opportunities for investment, makes her a power whose dependence upon worldwide peace and unhindered commerce is unique. Linguistically and culturally she remains somewhat apart from other advanced industrial nations in Western Europe and North America, but Japan is far more alien to Communist or Afro-Asian nations whose poverty, colonial past, and authoritarian regimes have little in common with the realities of contemporary Japan. Geographical and social distance may still separate Japan from the closest and most informal friendships of Western societies and Western statesmen, but political ideals and economic necessity demand increasing co-operation with the West and the firm establishment of a relationship based on mutual trust.

Bibliography

This list mentions some of the more recently published books which are likely to be available from libraries and bookshops.

General

BEASLEY, W. G. *The modern history of Japan* Weidenfeld and Nicolson, n.e. cased and paperback 1973.

BENEDICT, R. *The chrysanthemum and the sword: patterns of Japanese culture* Routledge and Kegan Paul, 1967; n.e. paperback 1977.

CHAMBERLAIN, B. H. *Things Japanese* Kegan Paul, 1890.

GIBNEY, F. *Japan: the fragile superpower* NY: Norton, n.e. 1979.

HEARN, L. *Japan: an attempt at interpretation* NY: Macmillan, 1904; Tokyo: Tuttle, 1955.

LIVINGSTONE, J. et al. *The Japan reader* Penguin Books, 2 vols. 1976.

REISCHAUER, E. O. *The Japanese* Harvard Univ. Press, 1977; n.e. paperback 1978.

RUDOFSKY, B. *The kimono mind* Gollancz, 1965.

SINGER, K. *Mirror, sword and jewel* ed. R. Storry. Croom Helm, 1973.

STORRY, R. *A history of modern Japan* Penguin Books, 1976.

VOGEL, E. F. *Japan as number one: lessons for America* Harvard Univ. Press, 1979.

Society

ABEGGLEN, J. C. *Management and worker: the Japanese solution* Kodansha International, US, 1978.

CLIFFORD, W. *Crime control in Japan* D. C. Heath, 1976.

COLE, R. E. *Japanese blue collar: the changing tradition* University of California Press, n.e. paperback 1973.

CUMMINGS, W. K. *Education and equality in Japan* Princeton University Press, cased and paperback 1980.

DORE, R. P. *British factory – Japanese factory* Allen and Unwin, cased and paperback 1973.

DORE, R. P. *City life in Japan: a study of a Tokyo ward* University of California Press, 1958; Routledge and Kegan Paul, 1958. op.

DORE, R. P. *Shinohata: a portrait of a Japanese village* Allen Lane, 1978.

FUKUTAKE, T. *Japanese society today* University of Tokyo Press, 1975.

HENDRY, J. *Marriage in changing Japan* Croom Helm, 1981.

KOBAYASHI, T. *Society, schools and progress in Japan* Pergamon Press, cased and paperback 1976.

LEBRA, J. et al. *Women in changing Japan* Stanford Univ. Press, paperback 1978.

NAKANE, C. *Japanese society* Weidenfeld and Nicolson, 1970. op; Penguin Books, 1973.

NORBECK, E. *Country to city: the urbanization of a Japanese hamlet* University of Utah Press, 1978.

OKOCHI, K. and KARSH, B. *Workers and employers in Japan* Princeton University Press, 1974.

PALMORE, E. *The honorable elders: a cross-cultural analysis of ageing in Japan* Duke University Press, 1975.

ROHLEN, T. P. *For harmony and strength: Japanese white collar organisation in anthropological perspective* University of California Press, 1974.

SHIMPO, M. *Three decades in Shiwa: economic development and social change in a Japanese farming community* University of British Columbia Press, 1977; Paul Norbury, 1978.

SINGLETON, J. C. *Nichu: a Japanese school* Holt, Rinehart, 1967.

SMITH, R. J. *Kurusu: the price of progress in a Japanese village, 1951–75* Stanford University Press, 1978.

VAN HELVOORT, E. *The Japanese working man: what choice? what reward?* Paul Norbury, 1979.

VOGEL, E. F. *Japan's new middle class: the salary man and his family in a Tokyo suburb* University of California Press, n.e. 1972.

de VOS, G. A. *Socialization for achievement: essays on the cultural psychology of the Japanese* University of California Press, 1973.

Young people

HENNY, S. *The role of women in modern Japanese society* Croom Helm, 1981.

KRAUSS, E. S. *Japanese radicals revisited: student protest in post-war Japan* University of California Press, 1974.

MASSEY, J. A. *Youth and politics in Japan* D. C. Heath, 1976.

MORLEY, J. W. ed. *Prologue to the future: the United States and Japan in the post-industrial age* D. C. Heath, 1974.

PHARR, S. J. *The Japanese woman: evolving views of life and role in Japan: the paradox of progress* ed. L. Austin. Yale University Press, 1976.

PLATH, D. W. ed. *Adult episodes in Japan* E. J. Brill, 1975.

Culture

BOCK, A. *Japanese film directors* Kodansha International: Phaidon Press, 1979.

BOWNAS, G. and THWAITE, A. eds. *The Penguin book of Japanese verse* Penguin Books, n.i. 1970.

BRANDON, J. R. ed. *Kabuki: five classic plays* Harvard University Press, 1975.

ERNST, E. *The Kabuki theatre* Oxford University Press, 1956; University Press of Hawaii, n.e. paperback 1974.

HILLIER, J. *Japanese colour prints* Phaidon Press, n.e. 1972.

ITO, T. *The Japanese garden: an approach to nature* Yale University Press, 1972.

KATO, S. *A history of Japanese literature: the first thousand years* Macmillan and Paul Norbury, 1980.

KEENE, D. *Anthology of Japanese literature* Allen and Unwin, 1956. op.; NY: Grove, paperback 1955.

KEENE, D. *Modern Japanese literature* Thames and Hudson, 1957. op.; NY: Grove, paperback 1956.

KEENE, D. *Twenty plays of the No theatre* Columbia University Press, paperback 1970.

LANE, R. *Images from the floating world: the Japanese print, including an illustrated dictionary of Ukiyo-e* Oxford University Press, 1978.

MELLEN, J. *The waves at Genji's door: Japan through its cinema* Pantheon, 1976.

PAINE, R. T. and SOPER, A. *The art and architecture of Japan* Penguin Books, 1955.

SANSOM, G. B. *Japan: a short cultural history* Barrie and Jenkins, n.i. 1976.

SCOTT, A. C. *The Kabuki theatre of Japan* Allen and Unwin, 1955.

SMITH, B. and KANAI, M. *Japan: a history in art* Weidenfeld and Nicolson, 1965.

SUZUKI, D. T. *Zen and Japanese culture* Routledge and Kegan Paul, 1959.

TIEDEMANN, A. E. *An introduction to Japanese civilisation* Columbia University Press, 1974; D. C. Heath, paperback 1974.

TUCKER, R. N. *Japan: film image* Studio Vista, 1973.

The following novels and short stories are also available in English:

ABE, K. *The woman in the dunes* Secker and Warburg, 1965. op.; Random House, 1972.

ABE, K. *Secret rendezvous* Knopf, 1979; Secker and Warburg, 1980.

AKUTAGAWA, R. *Kappa* Peter Owen, 1970; Greenwood, London, 1979

DAZAI, O. *The setting sun* Peter Owen, 1958; New Directions, paperback, 1968.

DAZAI, O. *No longer human* Peter Owen, 1959; New Directions, paperback, 1973.

ENDO, S. *The silence* Peter Owen, 1976; Quartet Books, 1978.

IBUSE, M. *Black rain* Secker and Warburg, 1971. op.; J. Martin, 1980.

KAWABATA, Y. *Snow country* Secker and Warburg, 1957. op.; Berkley Publ. n.d.

KAWABATA, Y. *Thousand cranes* Secker and Warburg, 1959. op.; NY: Knopf, 1969; Berkley Publ. n.d.

KAWABATA, Y. *The sound of the mountain* Secker and Warburg, 1971; Penguin Books, 1974.

KAWABATA, Y. *Beauty and sadness* Secker and Warburg, 1975; Penguin Books, 1979.

MISHIMA, Y. *The sound of waves* NY: Knopf, 1956; Berkley Publ., paperback, 1971; Secker and Warburg, 1957. op.

MISHIMA, Y. *The sailor who fell from grace with the sea and other stories* Secker and Warburg, 1966. op.; Penguin Books, 1970.

MISHIMA, Y. *Death in Midsummer and other stories* Secker and Warburg, 1967. op.; Penguin Books, 1971.

MISHIMA, Y. *Confessions of a mask* Peter Owen, 1960. op.; Panther, 1972.

MISHIMA, Y. *Spring snow* Secker and Warburg, 1972. op.; Penguin Books, 1976.

MISHIMA, Y. *Runaway horses* Secker and Warburg, 1973; Penguin Books, 1977.

MISHIMA, Y. *Temple of dawn* Secker and Warburg, 1974; Penguin Books, 1977.

MISHIMA, Y. *Decay of the angel* Secker and Warburg, 1975; Penguin Books, 1977.

OE, K. *A personal matter* NY: Grove, paperback, 1968; Weidenfeld and Nicolson, 1969. op.

OOKA, S. *Fires on the plain* Secker and Warburg, 1957. op.; Corgi, 1975; Greenwood US, 1978.

OSARAGI, J. *Homecoming* Secker and Warburg, 1955. op.; Greenwood, US, 1977.

SOSEKI, N. *Kokoro* Peter Owen, 1968.

SOSEKI, N. *Botchan* Peter Owen, 1973.

TANIZAKI, J. *Some prefer nettles* Secker and Warburg, 1956. op.; NY: Berkley Publ., 1975.

TANIZAKI, J. *The Makioka Sisters* Secker and Warburg, 1958. op.; NY: Knopf, 1957; Berkley Publ., paperback, 1975.

The economy

BLUMENTHAL, T. *Saving in post-war Japan* Harvard University Press, 1970.

BOLTHO, A. *Japan: an economic survey 1953–1973* Oxford University Press, cased and paperback 1976.

CLARK, R. *The Japanese company* Yale University Press, 1979.

FRANK, I. ed. *The Japanese economy in international perspective* Johns Hopkins University Press, cased and paperback 1975.

KERSHNER, T. R. *Japanese foreign trade* D. C. Heath, 1975.

MANNARI, H. *The Japanese business leaders* University of Tokyo Press, 1975.

MARSH, R. M. and MANNARI, H. *Modernisation and the Japanese factory* Princeton University Press, 1976.

OZAWA, T. *Japan's technological challenge to the West, 1950–1974* MIT Press, 1974.

SUZUKI, Y. *Money and banking in contemporary Japan* Yale University Press, 1980.

VOGEL, E. F. *Modern Japanese organisation and decision making* University of California Press, 1975.

YAMAMURA, K. *Economic policy in post-war Japan* University of California Press, 1968.

Politics

BAERWALD, H. H. *Japan's Parliament: an introduction* Cambridge Univ. Press, 1974.

CURTIS, G. L. *Election campaigning: Japanese style* Columbia University Press, 1971.

FUKUI, H. *Party in power: the Japanese Liberal Democrats and policy-making* University of California Press, 1970. op.

ITOH, H. *Japanese politics: an inside view* Cornell University Press, cased and paperback 1973.

PEMPEL, T. J. ed. *Policy-making in contemporary Japan* Cornell Univ. Press, 1977.

STOCKWIN, J. A. A. *Japan: divided politics in a growth economy* Weidenfeld and Nicolson, 1975.

THAYER, N. B. *How the Conservatives rule Japan* Princeton University Press, paperback 1969.

TSURUTANI, T. *Political change in Japan* Longman, paperback 1977.

WARD, R. E. *Japan's political system* Prentice-Hall, n.e. paperback 1968.

WATANUKI, J. *Politics in post-war Japanese society* University of Tokyo Press, 1977.

International relations

HANABUSA, M. *Trade problems between Japan and Western Europe* Saxon House for the RIIA, 1979.

HELLMAN, D. C. *Japan and East Asia: the new international order* Pall Mall, 1972.

KOJIMA, K. *Japan and a new world economic order* Croom Helm, 1977.

LANGDON, F. C. *Japan's foreign policy* University of British Columbia Press, 1974.

MENDL, W. *Issues in Japan's China policy* Macmillan, 1978.

OLSON, L. *Japan in post-war Asia* Pall Mall, 1970. op.

RIX, A. *Japan's economic aid* Croom Helm, 1980.

SCALAPINO, R. A. ed. *The foreign policy of modern Japan* University of California Press, 1977.

SWEARINGEN, R. *The Soviet Union and postwar Japan: escalating challenge and response* Stanford: Hoover Institutional Press, 1978.

WEINSTEIN, M. E. *Japan's post-war defense policy 1947–1968* Columbia University Press, 1971. op.

Acknowledgement is due to the following for permission to reproduce photographs:
ASSOCIATED PRESS demonstrations pages 71 and 72; BBC archives still from Rashomon page 120; JOHN BARROTT youths & girls page 63; MICHAEL DAUNCEY rice planting & country walk both page 33, Fuchu prison page 36 top, picnic page 85, Saihōji pages 106 & 107, calligrapher & Nō actor both page 125; FOREIGN PRESS CENTER, TOKYO school excursion page 56, Tokyo University page 74, Shinjuku page 131, flyovers page 134, Diet in session page 163, elections page 175, LDP party ballot page 181, press conference page 182, Cabinet page 184, Summit talks page 196, trade agreement page 201, Sino-Japanese treaty page 203, Chinese visit page 204, military parade page 212, Summit meeting page 215; FUJI BANK trainees page 76; LIBBY HALLIDAY Sumo wrestlers page 65, painting Daruma page 171 bottom; JAPAN INFORMATION CENTRE, LONDON surburban housing page 27, Danchi page 28, kindergarten page 50, Imperial Palace page 97, Nō play page 98, National Stadium Tokyo page 114, Tokyo cathedral page 115, flower arranging page 119 top, tea ceremony page 119 bottom, Diet building page 157, fishing fleets both page 199; JAPAN NATIONAL TOURIST ORGANISATION rice fields page 12, festival page 25, Tokyo station page 29, wedding page 43, Kendo class page 53, language laboratory page 54, Buddha page 92, koto players page 113, ship building page 145; MATSUSHITA ELECTRIC INDUSTRIAL CO assembling television sets pages 132 & 133; MITSUBISHI HEAVY INDUSTRIES company housing page 16, shipyard page 129, aircraft assembly line page 146; NATIONAL FILM ARCHIVE stills from Throne of Blood page 121, Gate of Hell page 122 top, Tokyo Story page 122 centre, Diary of a Shinjuku Thief page 122 bottom, Life of Oharu page 123; NHK TELEVISION pop show page 61; NISSAN MOTOR COMPANY LTD athletics day page 17, car factory page 137; ALAN SMITH basket weaver page 14, old people's home page 41, wedding page 42, Chinese delegation page 205; HOWARD SMITH Imperial Villa gardens, Katsura front cover, rice planting page 13, Nissan plant page 19, Sony factory girls page 20, prisoners working page 36 bottom, prison cells page 37, family meal page 47, young man page 62, McDonald's page 64 bottom, baseball team page 65 bottom, moss garden page 67 bottom, Shisendo page 68, Shintō priests page 91, garden & mosses pages 94 & 95, Yuize Shin'ichi page 113 top, agricultural machinery page 138, ship builders page 145, election posters and celebrations both page 159, displaying Daruma page 171 top, campaigning page 172; JOHN TELLICK Kabuki play page 101, making up page 104, fast foodstore page 142, demonstration page 160; WILLIAM TINGEY young woman's room page 30, shopping page 64 top, stone garden page 67 top, Love hotel page 82, cherry blossom page 126; ZEFA (photo R. Halin) Tokyo page 34.

Acknowledgement is also due to:
PENGUIN BOOKS LTD for extracts from *Penguin Book of Japanese Verse* in the English translation by Geoffrey Bownas and Anthony Thwaite.

Maps by Line and Line.

Index